GNOSIS AND THE NEW TESTAMENT

GNOSIS

AND THE

NEW TESTAMENT

R. McL. WILSON, B.D., Ph.D.

Senior Lecturer in New Testament
Language and Literature,
St. Mary's College,
University of St. Andrews

FORTRESS PRESS
PHILADELPHIA

Library of Congress Catalog No. 68–13446

Printed in Great Britain

Contents

Abbreviations

HTR	Harvard Theological Review
ICC	International Critical Commentary
JEH	Journal of Ecclesiastical History
JTS	Journal of Theological Studies
NTS	New Testament Studies
OLZ	Orientalistische Literaturzeitung
PW	Pauly-Wissowa-Kroll, *Realenzyklopaedie*
RAC	*Reallexikon f. Antike u. Christentum*
RGG	*Die Religion in Geschichte u. Gegenwart*
RoB	Religion och Bibel
ThR	Theologische Rundschau
TLZ	Theologische Literaturzeitung
TU	Texte u. Untersuchungen
TWB	Theologisches Wörterbuch zum NT
Vig.Chr.	Vigiliae Christianae
ZKG	Zeitschrift f. Kirchengeschichte
ZKT	Zeitschrift f. katholische Theologie
ZNW	Zeitschrift f. neutestamentliche Wissenschaft
ZRGG	Zeitschrift f. Religions- u. Geistesgeschichte
ZTK	Zeitschrift f. Theologie u. Kirche

Preface

THIS book had its origin in a series of lectures delivered in the spring of 1965 at a number of universities and colleges in the United States and Canada. My wife and I have the most pleasant memories of our extended tour, and we should like to take this opportunity of expressing our thanks to all those who by the warmth of their welcome and cordial hospitality helped to make our journey so enjoyable. To mention a few however, and ignore the others, would be invidious and ungracious; but the list is frankly too long to print, the more especially if it were extended, as it ought to be, to include not only the institutions but the individuals who received us so warmly. We therefore hope our American and Canadian friends will accept this general expression of our thanks and appreciation.

One name however must be mentioned, that of the late Professor Kendrick Grobel, who was responsible for the initial invitation which enabled me to spend a semester as Visiting Professor at Vanderbilt Divinity School, and who later crowned all the many kindnesses he and Mrs. Grobel showed us by planning and arranging the whole tour for us. It was our one regret that his untimely death just before we set out made it impossible for us to report to him on our return how well his plans had been laid.

For publication, the lectures have been completely revised and considerably expanded. In chapter 5 in particular opportunity has been taken to include some discussion of the significance of each of the documents so far published. The lecture form has however been preserved so far as possible, and detailed technical discussion therefore avoided. References to the relevant literature are supplied in the footnotes, but no attempt has been made at a complete coverage. Detailed analysis of differing points of view would have extended the book far beyond the limits of space available.

An earlier version of chapter 4 appeared as an article in the *Expository Times*, and I have to thank the editor for granting permission for the use of this material here. Dr. Ernest Best and Mr. G. E. McMillan read the manuscript, and have helped to eliminate various weaknesses, but are not of course responsible for any shortcomings which remain. Finally, my thanks are due to Mrs. Isobel Stuart, who efficiently reduced a not always very tidy manuscript to neat and orderly pages of type.

St. Mary's College,   R. McL. Wilson
St. Andrews
January 1967

I

The Gnostic Heresy in the Light of
Recent Research and Discovery

I N the Kerr Lectures delivered in the University of Glasgow in
1909, Dr. Robert Law observed that the rise and spread of
Gnosticism 'forms one of the dimmest chapters in Church history.'[1] Even today it would be too much to say that the
obscurity has been altogether removed, the darkness dissipated.
We cannot yet trace the whole history of this movement in all its
ramifications, or identify the precise influences which were
operative at each particular stage of its development. Nevertheless progress has been made. The patient study and research of
many scholars, and the discovery of quite substantial quanties
of new material, have shed light on many a dark corner and
contributed to a fuller and better understanding. But, as so
often happens, the removal of one problem has sometimes only
given rise to several others. New discoveries have provided the
answers to some of our questions, but in their turn they have
raised new questions for investigation, questions of dating,
questions of relationship to the material already known, or to
the other documents contained in these new discoveries themselves, and so on. New methods of research again have prompted
the reconsideration of many problems, but the new solutions
offered have not always proved entirely satisfactory.[2]

The extent of the progress that has been made may perhaps
be most readily seen from a consideration of Francis Legge's
Forerunners and Rivals of Christianity, which has recently appeared
in a second edition.[3] First published in 1915 in two volumes,
this is in many ways an excellent book, and no disparagement is

---

[1] Robert Law, *The Tests of Life*, (Edinburgh 1909), p. 26.
[2] For a recent survey see K. Rudolph, 'Stand u. Aufgaben in der
Erforschung des Gnostizismus', Tagung f. Allgemeine Religionsgeschichte
1963, Sonderheft der *Wiss. Zeitschr. Jena*, pp. 89 ff.
[3] F. Legge, *Fore-runners and Rivals of Christianity*, (2 vols., Cambridge 1915;
reprinted in one vol., New York 1964).

intended when it is used in the present connection. Its author was a scholar, with a truly scholarly and scientific approach—if anything perhaps rather ahead of his time. His descriptions of the actual documents which were available to him are still useful and accurate, and much may be learned from his work. The second edition however is a reprint, unchanged and without revision, of the 1915 book, and therefore suffers from the simple fact that it is fifty years out of date, for much has happened in the interval. In his chapter on Manicheism, for example, Legge refers to the Turfan fragments, at that time a comparatively recent discovery; but he had of course no knowledge of the Coptic Manichean documents which only became available in the thirties.[4] To the Mandeans, again, he makes only passing reference, for he wrote before the 'Mandean fever' of the twenties, and without access even to the earliest Mandean documents to be published; but in some quarters there has been a tendency among modern scholars to treat Mandeism almost as normative for the study of Gnosticism.[5] Thirdly, and here again he was in advance of his time, Legge speaks of pre-Christian Gnostics, although he was well aware that in so doing he was widening the range of the term. Many scholars today would agree, but not all would approve of his choice—the Orphics, the Essenes and Simon Magus.[6]

Simon, of course, is denounced by Irenaeus as 'the father of all heresies', and the question whether he should be included here is to some extent one of definition: was he a Gnostic, and in what sense, before he came into contact with Christianity? And how far can the teachings of the later Simonian sect be attributed to the founder? In the other two cases, however, Legge had to make his bricks with a rather scanty minimum of straw—in the case of the Essenes on the basis of the information

[4] H. J. Polotsky, *Manichäische Homilien*, (Stuttgart 1934); H. J. Polotsky and A. Böhlig, *Kephalaia*, (Stuttgart 1940); C. R. C. Allberry, *A Manichean Psalm-Book*, (Stuttgart 1938). See also Polotsky, art. Manichäismus in *PW* Suppt. VI; Böhlig, *Wiss. Zeitschr. Halle* X.1, (1961), pp. 157 ff. K. Rudolph, *Wiss. Zeitschr. Halle* (Sonderheft 1965), pp. 156 ff.

[5] Cf. Schmithals' criticism of Jonas in *Die Gnosis in Korinth*, (Göttingen 1956), p. 87 n.1.

[6] For Orphism, cf. U. Bianchi, *Numen* 12, (1965), pp. 161 ff.; for Simon, E. Haenchen, *Gott und Mensch*, (Tübingen 1965), pp. 265 ff. [=*ZTK* 49, (1952), pp. 316 ff.].

supplied by Philo and Josephus, with the assistance of a certain amount of imagination. He had of course no knowledge of Qumran, and the scrolls which have shed so much fresh light upon a hitherto almost unknown aspect of Judaism in the New Testament period. In this connection it may be noted that when the Dead Sea Scrolls were first discovered many claimed that this was the library of a Gnostic sect; but these claims soon subsided.[7] As it has been said, nearly all the ingredients of the later Gnosticism are present,[8] yet something still is missing. The Scrolls are important for the study of Gnosticism, as they are important for the New Testament period as a whole, particularly from the point of view of the Jewish background. But here again there is a question of definition, to which we must return. At these three points then, Manicheism, Mandeism and Essenism, we now have at our disposal a mass of documentary evidence, some of it not yet fully evaluated, of which Legge and his contemporaries never knew; and this takes no account of the specifically Gnostic texts which have now become available, or of the research that has been done by many scholars.

Looking back across the years, we can trace a distinct change in the estimates of Gnosticism which have been put forward, from the somewhat contemptuous disparagement of Charles Bigg,[9] who wrote of the Gnostics 'the ordinary Christian controversialist felt that he had nothing to do but set out at unsparing length their tedious pedigrees, in the well-grounded confidence that no-one would care to peruse them a second time', to the more complimentary opinions which saw in them the first real theologians, the men who for all their shortcomings first grappled with the problems of presenting the Gospel in adequate philosophical terms and who by their very errors forced the Church to the elaboration of a more satisfactory solution. Bigg might have paused to consider that Irenaeus and Hippolytus, to name no others, both wrote at considerable length against the Gnostics—which at least suggests that to them this movement was a serious threat; otherwise they would not have put themselves to so much trouble.

But what *is* Gnosticism and who were the Gnostics? As

---

[7] Cf. Wilson, *The Gnostic Problem*, (London 1958), pp. 73 f.

[8] R. M. Grant, *Gnosticism and Early Christianity*, (New York 1959), p. 39.

[9] Charles Bigg, *The Christian Platonists of Alexandria*, (Oxford 1886), p. 28.

Bultmann puts it,[10] Gnosticism 'first appeared and attracted the attention of scholars as a movement within the Christian religion, and for a long time it was regarded as a purely Christian movement, a perversion of the Christian faith into a speculative theology.' The various Gnostic systems described by the early Fathers differ on points of detail, but the basic elements common to them all are (1) a distinction between the unknown and transcendent true God on the one hand and the Demiurge or creator of this world on the other, the latter being commonly identified with the God of the Old Testament; (2) the belief that man in his true nature is essentially akin to the divine, a spark of the heavenly light imprisoned in a material body and subjected in this world to the dominance of the Demiurge and his powers; (3) a myth narrating some kind of pre-mundane fall, to account for man's present state and his yearning for deliverance; and (4) the means, the saving *gnosis*, by which that deliverance is effected and man awakened to the consciousness of his own true nature and heavenly origin. This deliverance, and the eventual return of the imprisoned sparks of light to their heavenly abode, means in time the return of this world to its primordial chaos, and is strenuously opposed at all points by the hostile powers.

Some elements of Gnostic thought are shared by other religious movements also. Moreover, as van Unnik says,[11] 'the Gnostics often applied the principle of "Je prends mon bien où je le trouve" ', taking over and adapting for their own purposes the ideas, the language and sometimes the literature of other faiths. It is this that creates the problem first of defining Gnosticism in such a way as to cover all that is essentially Gnostic, without at the same time including elements common to Gnosticism and to other faiths which are not necessarily essentially Gnostic at all; and secondly of determining the origins and development of this movement, and the influences which were operative in the process. As will become apparent later, it

[10] Rudolf Bultmann, *Primitive Christianity in its Contemporary Setting*, (ET: London 1956), p. 162. The German original has 'die Gnosis', which in this context implies something rather wider than 'Gnosticism' as understood by most English-speaking scholars (see below).

[11] W. C. van Unnik, *Newly Discovered Gnostic Documents*, (ET: London 1960), p. 91.

is not the separate elements in themselves which are Gnostic, but the total synthesis, the system, into which they are combined.

The traditional theory, which in general held its ground from Irenaeus down to the time of Harnack, saw in Gnosticism a Christian heresy, the result of the contamination of the faith by the muddy waters of Greek philosophy. Thus Harnack in a famous phrase spoke of 'the acute hellenisation of Christianity.'[12] Plotinus, one must suspect, would have demurred—for him the contamination was the adulteration of the pure stream of Platonic philosophy by the new-fangled Christian faith. From Harnack's point of view the whole history of early Christianity, from the beginnings down to the time of Nicaea, is one of hellenisation. Gnosticism marks an *acute* hellenisation, the difference in some sense being no more than one of degree. Towards the end of the nineteenth century, however, and in the course of the twentieth, a different view prevails. No longer are the Gnostics in the van of progress—on the contrary, they belong to the forces of reaction. They represent not the pioneers of Christian theology but almost the last resistance of the ancient world to the triumph of Christianity. Gnosticism, on this view, is not merely a deviation from Christianity but a recrudescence and resurgence of ancient Oriental religion, indeed a religion in its own right, invading the West as the rival and competitor of the Christian faith. And this view has claimed the allegiance of a considerable body of scholars, from Reitzenstein and Bousset down to Bultmann and his pupils.[13] But it has not gone without its opponents.

One difficulty lies in the fact that it has proved impossible to identify one single source from which the movement could be said to take its origin. A religion is normally the faith of a particular people, although in course of time it may come to be propagated also in other lands and among other peoples, as with Judaism or the mystery religions; or it may take its rise from a particular founder within an existing tradition, as with

---

[12] A. von Harnack, *History of Dogma*, i, (ET: London 1897), p. 226. Cf. R. P. Casey in *JTS* 36, (1935), pp. 45 ff.

[13] Cf. Carsten Colpe, *Die religionsgeschichtliche Schule*, (Göttingen 1961), and for Bultmann his *Primitive Christianity* [n. 10 above]. See also H. Langerbeck, *Aufsätze zur Gnosis*, (Göttingen 1967).

Buddhism, Christianity and Islam. In either case we can identify the milieu and the point of origin, but with Gnosticism this is not the case. Numerous candidates have been nominated—Egypt, Babylonia, Persia, the hellenised Judaism of Alexandria. The explanation has been sought in philosophy and in magic, in the mystery religions, and in the disappointed eschatological hopes of early Christians or of Qumran sectarians. All too often Reitzenstein's warning[14] has gone unheeded—that the individual scholar almost inevitably tends to fall victim to a kind of colour blindness, which makes him insensitive to important distinctions, and that according to the direction of his own specialised studies each tends to give undue significance to particular aspects; which can only mean a distorted picture of the whole. But few today in this age of specialisation can claim the necessary mastery in all the disciplines involved—classical and Biblical scholarship, Egyptology, *Iranistik*, the lore of ancient Babylon and Mesopotamia, not to mention the underworld of alchemy and magic, or the literatures of Qumran and Gnosticism, Manicheism and Mandeism. As Reitzenstein said, only the combined work of many can bring us to a real solution.

In point of fact, Gnosticism is fundamentally syncretistic, welding into a new synthesis elements from diverse cultures. It would be more correct to recognise the various 'spheres of influence' mentioned[15] as the *ultimate* sources of particular ideas, and proceed to the attempt to trace the channels by which they passed into the developed Gnostic systems. It should be added that, as Jonas pointed out,[16] Gnosticism is not *merely* syncretism, or syncretism Gnosis. To quote Bultmann again,[17] 'the essence of Gnosticism does not lie in its syncretistic mythology but rather in a new understanding—new in the ancient world—of man and the world.'

A second difficulty lies in our present lack of an agreed terminology. The terms *gnosis*, Gnostic and Gnosticism were for centuries employed to describe the Christian heresy—although even this was in fact an extension of the original meaning: it is

---

[14] R. Reitzenstein, *Poimandres*, (Leipzig 1904), p. 250; cf. C. H. Dodd, *The Bible and the Greeks*, (London 1935), p. xv.

[15] The phrase is van Unnik's (op. cit. p. 35).

[16] Hans Jonas, *Gnosis u. spätantiker Geist*, i, (Göttingen ²1954), pp. 77 ff.

[17] Bultmann, *Theology of the NT*, i, (ET: London 1952), p. 165.

the *gnosis* falsely so called that Irenaeus assails, and only some of the heretical groups described by the early Fathers claimed the name. A *gnosis* falsely so called carries with it the implication that there is a true *gnosis*, so that we are faced at once with the problem of finding terms by which to distinguish them. In modern research the extension has been carried further still. German scholars in particular have widened the horizon, noting in the first place that the phenomena which appear in the Christian heresy do not stand alone, for similar phenomena can be seen elsewhere, outside of Christianity; and secondly that there are certain affinities earlier, for example in the New Testament itself, in the writings of Philo of Alexandria, or in the scrolls from Qumran. The consequence has been, inevitably, a certain amount of confusion and misunderstanding, arising from the use of the same terms in different senses. In the field of *Dogmengeschichte*, Gnosticism is still for many writers the heresy of the second century, whereas in that of *Religionsgeschichte* 'Gnosis' is something very much wider and more comprehensive, so much so indeed that some scholars appear unable to see anything but Gnosis when they investigate the background of the New Testament or even the New Testament documents themselves. A further complication arises from the use of the phenomenological as distinct from the historical approach. When we are studying the phenomena we have to note the similarities, the typical features, but these similarities do not necessarily guarantee any historical continuity, a point that has not always been borne in mind. From the phenomenological point of view it may be perfectly legitimate to group religious movements together on the basis of their common elements; but this does not necessarily mean that these movements stand in any genetic relationship, or that there is any direct connection between the earlier and the later.

English-speaking scholars on the whole have tended to adhere to the traditional definition. F. C. Burkitt for example urged that the best way in which to approach the second century systems was to regard them as Christian systems, and his arguments for the essential Christianity of Valentinus were accepted as convincing by C. H. Dodd.[18] Dodd in his turn explicitly

[18] F. C. Burkitt, *Church and Gnosis*, (Cambridge 1932); C. H. Dodd, *The Interpretation of the Fourth Gospel*, (Cambridge 1953), p. 100 n.4.

recognised that there is a sense in which the wider definition employed by German scholars is apposite, but he himself held to the narrower definition. Within recent years R. P. Casey[19] has developed a lengthy attack on the idea that a vaguely defined and widespread Gnosis had anything to do with the origins of Christianity. In this connection Dodd[20] noted three points which are worthy of being kept in mind:

1. There is no Gnostic document known to us which can with any show of probability be dated—at any rate in the form in which alone we have access to it—before the period of the New Testament.

2. The typical Gnostic systems all combine in various ways and proportions ideas derived from Christianity with ideas which can be shown to be derived from, or at least to have affinities with, other religious or philosophical traditions.

3. The various Gnostic systems differ widely in the way in which they introduce and combine these disparate elements, and each system has to be considered separately for what it is in itself. No general and all-embracing answer can be given to the question, What is the relation of Gnosticism to Christianity?

Nevertheless English-speaking scholars have tended more and more towards some acceptance of the German point of view—albeit with certain reservations. Thus in a recent article, published posthumously, the late A. D. Nock[21] can expressly recognise the existence of 'a gnostic way of thinking' in the period prior to the New Testament, although he also says that the relation of the Gospel of Truth and other recently discovered texts to the New Testament seems 'to vindicate completely the traditional view of Gnosticism as Christian heresy with roots in speculative thought.'

Our first requirement then at the present time is clarity and precision of definition, some measure of agreement as to what we mean by the terms we use. One possible solution is to distinguish

---

[19] *The Background of the NT and its Eschatology*, ed. W. D. Davies and D. Daube, (Cambridge 1956), pp. 52 ff.

[20] *Interpretation*, p. 98.

[21] *HTR* 57, (1964), pp. 255 ff. [quotation from p. 276].

between Gnosticism on the one hand and Gnosis on the other. By Gnosticism we mean the specifically Christian heresy of the second century A.D., by Gnosis, in a broader sense, the whole complex of ideas belonging to the Gnostic movement and related trends of thought. A difficulty here is the fact that we have only the one adjective 'Gnostic' to do duty for both purposes. Something can be done by use of modifications such as 'pre-gnostic', 'semi-gnostic' or 'gnosticising'; but here again such terms are not always clearly defined or precisely used. Worst of all, sometimes a term or concept, a theme or idea, is described as 'Gnostic' because as a matter of fact it does appear in Gnosticism as more narrowly defined. But having used the term *descriptively* and noted that this 'Gnostic' theme or concept occurs in the New Testament, the author then proceeds as if it had been used *derivatively*—to claim the point as evidence of Gnostic 'influence' upon some New Testament writer. We need to bear in mind here the warning, neatly phrased by E. Earle Ellis,[22] against the tendency 'to convert parallels into influences and influences into sources.' Also we need to pay greater attention to questions of chronology, for sometimes it would appear that scholars have formulated a synthesis on the basis of second or third century sources, and have then proceeded to force the New Testament writings into the resultant mould, on the assumption that the hypothetical pre-Christian gnosis which they postulate was identical with their reconstruction from the later documents.

This question of a pre-Christian Gnosticism is one that has been long and hotly debated. On the one hand Alan Richardson[23] says 'the objection to speaking of Gnosticism in the first century A.D. is that we are in danger of hypostatising certain rather ill-defined tendencies of thought and then speaking as if there were a religion or religious philosophy, called Gnosticism, which could be contrasted with Judaism or Christianity. There was of course no such thing.' On the other hand some scholars would argue that even if the tendencies of thought are rather ill-defined the very fact that similar motifs and conceptions appear in so many different areas, and in so many distinct systems, points to a common source on which they all depend.

[22] *Paul's Use of the Old Testament*, (Edinburgh 1957), p. 82.
[23] *An Introduction to the Theology of the NT*, (London 1958), p. 41.

B

Giovanni Miegge[24] writes 'pre-Christian Gnosticism may be, in reality, nothing more than an unknown something postulated by the science of religions, one of those invisible stars the position of which astronomers determine by calculating the deviations in the movements of neighbouring stars.'

On this two things require to be said: first, this is a brilliant analogy, but analogies can be misleading. The planet Uranus, which was actually discovered in the position calculated by the astronomers, is a solid mass which was already there and able to exert a gravitational pull upon its neighbours. We have no grounds for assuming that the analogy holds in the realm of thought and ideas for, secondly, Miegge goes on to quote a passage from Bultmann:[25] 'Even though the ideas have to be worked out in the mass and in detail from documents which are later than the Gospel according to St. John, that the ideas themselves date back to a period prior to the Gospel remains certain, beyond a shadow of doubt.' Now it is a fact that particular ideas can be traced far back into the pre-Christian period to ultimate origins in Egypt or Babylon or Persia. But were these ideas already Gnostic in the lands of their origin, or at what point do they become Gnostic? Here it seems there is a real possibility of clarifying our procedure if we think in terms of growth and development. The ideas admittedly are pre-Christian but the combination of these ideas, the way in which they are blended together, the associations which they come to have, these may only be Gnostic in the context of specifically Gnostic systems, which would mean that the ideas themselves are not necessarily Gnostic. The Gnostics adapted to their own ends the material they took over, and it is no small part of our problem to determine whether at any given point a particular term or concept carries the Gnostic connotation, whether in the New Testament, for example, a word which is a technical term in the second-century Gnostic systems should be given a Gnostic meaning, or whether this Gnostic meaning is in fact a secondary development.

At the present time there is a broad consensus of opinion over a fairly wide area of research. It is on points of detail that the

[24] *Gospel and Myth*, (ET: London 1960), p. 30.
[25] *Das Evangelium des Johannes*, pp. 11–12 [the translation is that of Miegge's translator, Bishop Stephen Neill].

differences emerge—on questions of origins and development, on the precise relation of one element to another. Where did this conception or that originate? How and why was it brought into its present context? What is its present significance and is this the significance it has always had, or has it at some point in the process undergone a change, and if so why and under what influences? Such are the questions which are being raised and must be raised; but sometimes we are not yet in a position to give a final answer.

To begin with Gnosticism as traditionally defined, we have long known enough about its general character for the purposes of the history of doctrine, enough to define it in a manual of Church history or in a dictionary of theology as the result of the amalgamation of Christianity and paganism, one consequence of the emergence of Christianity upon the stage of the wider world of the Roman empire, which carried with it the necessity for the reinterpretation of the original Palestinian gospel in language 'understanded of the people', in terms comprehensible to men and women of Gentile origin and background who had no real roots in the Old Testament and Jewish tradition. So much is clear and would be generally agreed. But was Gnosticism fundamentally Christian or essentially pagan? Does it owe more to the essential truths of the Gospel or to the ideas of the pagan world? Here there might be less agreement. If we think in terms of particular Gnostics and ask whether they were Christians who sought, as Burkitt said,[26] to present their faith in terms more acceptable to their own enlightened age, or pagans who sought to claim something of this new and potent Christian religion for their own purposes, we should have to say in general that some were one and some the other; when we endeavour to deal with Gnosticism in the abstract it is much more difficult. In the light of recent studies it is even open to question whether we should think in terms only of Christianity and paganism. As will appear, the Jewish element in Gnostic thought is sufficiently prominent to lead some scholars to think of a Jewish origin for the whole movement.

Again, how are we to distinguish between the Christian Gnosticism which is orthodox, or comparatively orthodox, in

[26] Cf. *Church and Gnosis*, pp. 27 f.

Clement of Alexandria and Origen, and the Christian Gnosticism which is heretical in Basilides or in Valentinus? What are we to make of the affinities which exist between the heretical Gnostic systems attacked by Irenaeus on the one hand and the Corpus Hermeticum on the other, or such fragments as we possess from the middle Platonism of the second century, or the neo-Platonism of Plotinus?[27] If these affinities suggest that the traditional theory is correct in seeing Gnosticism as the contamination of Christianity by philosophy, what of the affinities with the magical papyri, or with the mystery religions, or with astrology? If we are to think in terms of philosophy, again, at what stage did Christianity rise to such a level of society as to make influence from philosophy in the proper sense conceivable? It is scarcely within the New Testament period, for there is little there to compare with what we find in a Clement or an Origen —yet there are affinities with the later Gnostic heresy within the New Testament itself, as also in a contemporary writer like Philo of Alexandria.[28] When we add the indisputable similarities in Manicheism or in the Mandean literature, and at the other end what appear to be certain tendencies in the direction of Gnosticism in the Qumran texts, it becomes apparent that we can no longer think solely in terms of the second century or in terms of Gnosticism and Christianity. We have to set the whole problem in a very much wider context and consider it in the light of what we know or what we can learn about the whole religious situation and its developments in the early Christian centuries, and it is precisely here that the difficulties and the differences of opinion begin to emerge.

Manicheism, for example, originated in Persia in the third century A.D., although many elements in Manichean thought can be traced back a great deal further.[29] In particular the dualism that is so characteristic of Gnostic thinking may be very

[27] For Plotinus, cf. J. Zandee, *The Terminology of Plotinus and of Some Gnostic Writings*, (Ned. Hist.-Archaeol. Inst. Istanbul, 1961). Cf. also, for a wider field, E. R. Dodds, *Pagan and Christian in an Age of Anxiety*, (Cambridge 1965).

[28] For Philo, cf. Wilson, *The Gnostic Problem*; also the paper by M. Simon at the Messina Colloquium 1966 [see below].

[29] Cf. Geo. Widengren, *Mani and Manicheism*, (ET: London 1965); A. Adam in *Hbuch der Orientalistik*, viii. 2, (Leiden 1961), pp. 102 ff. H. C. Puech, *Le Manichéisme. Son fondateur, sa doctrine*, (Paris 1949).

plausibly linked with the dualism in the teaching of Zoroaster centuries before the birth of Christ. Hence when other elements in the Gnostic and Manichean tradition were also found in Zoroastrian texts it was but natural to think of a Persian origin for the whole movement and to attempt to trace the spread of its influence to the West. But, for one thing, there are different kinds of dualism, and a dualistic system is not for that reason necessarily Gnostic. For another, Zoroastrianism itself had a history. It is at least debatable whether some of these ideas already belonged to it in the pre-Christian period, or owe their presence to some extraneous influence. An idea, for example, which does not occur in the earliest Zoroastrian literature, but only in texts dating from the Sassanid period in the third century A.D. or later, cannot be seriously claimed in evidence for Zoroastrian influence on the thinking of an earlier age. Nor can we assume that the influence was always exerted from the one side and in the same direction. An example here is provided by a paper read at the Messina Colloquium on the origins of Gnosticism in 1966 by Dr. Edward Conze,[30] in which he drew attention to a number of parallels between Gnosticism and Mahayana Buddhism. At certain points, however, Dr. Conze was prepared to admit the possibility of Gnostic influence upon Buddhism, not the reverse. We have to allow for the possibility that influences moved in both directions, not only from East to West, but also from West to East. And we have further to consider whether the same words, the same phrases, the same concepts, have always and in every case the same associations and the same special meaning.

The Mandeans again still survive in the regions of Iraq and Iran, but their tradition claims an origin in the first century A.D. in the area of the Jordan valley.[31] We know something of 'Baptist' sects in that region in the early centuries,[32] and here

[30] For reports of the Colloqium see U. Bianchi, *Numen* 13, (1966), pp. 151 ff.; G. W. MacRae, *Catholic Biblical Quarterly* 28, (1966), pp. 322 ff. The papers submitted have now been published: *Le Origini dello Gnosticismo*, ed. U. Bianchi [Suppt. xii to *Numen*, (Leiden 1967)].

[31] See E. S. Drower, *The Secret Adam*, (Oxford 1960); K. Rudolph, *Die Mandäer*, (vol. 1, Göttingen 1960; vol. 2, 1961); id., *Theogonie, Cosmogonie und Anthropogonie in den mandäischen Schriften*, (Göttingen 1965).

[32] Cf. J. Thomas, *Le mouvement baptiste en Palestine et Syrie*, (Gembloux 1935).

again it was natural for scholars to seek an origin and an explanation for the whole movement on the basis of the Mandeans. It was this that occasioned the 'Mandean fever' of the twenties, a fever which abated when Lietzmann on the one hand pointed out that Mandean documents showed a knowledge of later Syrian liturgies and Burkitt on the other indicated their acquaintance with the Peshitta.[33] Thereafter interest in the Mandeans rather subsided, but recently it has been revived again. In several quarters it has been affirmed that the question is not yet closed, and this may well be so. Indeed the points made by Lietzmann and Burkitt may have a different significance—not as grounds for dismissing the Mandeans altogether, but as warnings of the need for care and caution in the drawing of our conclusions. It is perfectly possible that the Mandean tradition is correct, that the distant ancestors of this group did in fact migrate from the Jordan valley; but at some stage they were influenced by the Syrian church. We must therefore ask: to what other influences have they been subjected in the course of their lengthy history? How much of Mandean tradition as it now stands in the documents of their literature goes back in fact to the days of their origin, and how much is later accretion? Again, can we detect the stages at which such accretion took place? Manicheism and Mandeism have much to teach us, but we must beware of the facile assumption that what we find in them was there from the very outset. It is not difficult to imagine a group like that represented by the Dead Sea Scrolls migrating in the course of the first century, adopting some elements of the teaching of Marcion or of Gnosticism in the second, or of Manicheism in the third, reacting violently against persecution by more 'orthodox' neighbours at another stage, and finally emerging after several centuries with a collection of treasured documents which to some extent reflected their chequered history, but were no longer fully understood even by

[33] H. Lietzmann, *Kleine Schriften*, i, (*TU* 67, Berlin 1958), pp. 124 ff. (=SB Berlin 1930, pp. 596 ff.); F. C. Burkitt, *JTS* 29, (1928), pp. 235 ff., and *Church and Gnosis*, p. 106. Cf. W. F. Albright, *From the Stone Age to Christianity*, (Baltimore 1957), pp. 364 ff.; G. Bornkamm, *Jesus of Nazareth*, (ET: London 1960), p. 198 n.34; Cullmann, *Christology of the NT*, (ET: London 1963), p. 27 n.1, and the literature there cited.

the wisest of their number. [34] In such a case the problem would be to isolate the different stages, to recognise the influences which have operated at one period or another, and to determine when the common elements are to be taken as indications of extraneous influence upon our hypothetical group, when that group itself has influenced some other body, and when both groups are dependent not upon one another but upon some third source that lies behind them both.

Here attention should be drawn to a point that has not always received sufficient notice: that Gnosticism grew. It is, I believe, a fundamental mistake to think of the whole movement emerging in all the glory of its final development, or to assume that where one or two elements of later Gnostic thought, or even several elements, are present then the whole range is already there. To revert to the analogy of ingredients, already mentioned, a visit to the kitchen will soon disclose that even the assembling of all the necessary ingredients does not necessarily produce the finished dish. They may still require to be blended together in the proper proportions, and the mixture cooked; and the presence or absence of a single ingredient, or some variation in the quantities used, or in the method of mixing employed, may make a very considerable difference to the finished product. Gnosticism grew. Our problem therefore is to trace the process of its growth, from the earliest discernible origins to the full development in the sects of the second century and on to Manicheism and Mandeism, and from these again down through the related sects of the Middle Ages, the Bogomils, the Cathari, the Albigensians. [35] In so doing we shall have to recognise affinities outside the Gnostic tradition proper, in Christianity, for example, on the one hand, in Jewish mysticism on the other. There is a sense in which we may rightly speak of 'gnosis' as something much wider than the second century Christian

[34] Cf. R. Macuch, *TLZ* 1957, cols. 401 ff., 1965, cols. 649 ff.; K. Rudolph, *Die Mandäer*, i, pp. 252 ff.

[35] Cf. D. Obolensky, *The Bogomils*, (Cambridge 1948); S. Runciman, *The Medieval Manichee*, (Cambridge 1947), and for Jewish Cabbalism the works of G. Scholem. In this connection it may be as well to recall the warning voiced at the Messina Colloquium by H. Jonas against the assumption of a 'conveyor-belt' development. It is not merely a process of addition, but also of modification and adaptation, and sometimes of omission.

heresy, something of an atmosphere in which the people of the early Christian centuries lived and moved, but we must beware of assuming too readily that this 'gnosis' was in all respects and at all stages identical with the specifically heretical Christian Gnosticism of the second century schools, and we must give due regard to the mutual interaction of many different traditions.[36] We have to take account of Jews like Philo, Christians like Clement and Origen, Gnostics like Valentinus—and also of a host of others. Sweeping generalisations are out of place—on the contrary we have need of detailed and meticulous study of particular theories, of the ideas of individual thinkers, of the systems of particular schools.

Here in fact a great deal has already been done in the analysis and interpretation of the information provided by the early Fathers. There was a period at which it could be suggested that their evidence must be considered suspect, since it came from the opponents of the Gnostics, men whose concern it was to refute the Gnostic theories in the interest of what later came to be the Catholic faith; and indeed there are certain Fathers whose statements must occasionally be received with a due measure of caution. But the general reliability of Irenaeus, our earliest major witness, has been abundantly vindicated by the researches of Foerster and Sagnard,[37] and the conclusions of these scholars are now amply confirmed by such of the Nag Hammadi documents as have been published. Irenaeus may not always have understood his opponents, and certainly he was not always in sympathy with them, but it cannot be said that he deliberately misinterpreted them in the interest of his own polemic.

At this point further reference should be made to the Messina Colloquium in 1966, at which a large gathering of scholars and

[36] The late Johannes Munck suggested the substitution of 'syncretism' for 'gnosis' in this wider sense [*Current Issues in the NT*, ed. Klassen and Snyder, (London 1962), p. 236], but while I am in complete sympathy with his aim and purpose I cannot consider the suggestion satisfactory. The term 'syncretism' is already employed in two distinct though related senses, which has led to considerable confusion. To add a third shade of meaning would only make confusion worse confounded.

[37] W. Foerster, *Von Valentin zu Heracleon*, (Beiheft 7 zur *ZNW*, Giessen 1928); F. M. M. Sagnard, *La gnose valentinienne et le témoignage de S. Irénée*, (Paris 1947).

specialists from many countries met to discuss the problems of the origins of Gnosticism.[38] One feature of this meeting was a number of papers underlining the Jewish contribution to Gnostic thought. Another was the attempt made to formulate a definition of Gnosticism, to clarify the whole situation and eliminate the problems arising from failures of definition. This definition began from the classic Gnosticism of the second century and distinguished Gnosticism in this sense from 'gnosis', which is defined as 'knowledge of the divine mysteries reserved for an elect'. The Gnosticism of the second century sects 'involves a coherent series of characteristics which can be summed up in the idea of a divine spark in man, deriving from the divine realm, fallen into this world of fate, birth and death, and needing to be awakened by the divine counterpart of the self in order to be finally reintegrated.' It was noted that not every gnosis is Gnosticism, 'but only that which involves in this perspective the idea of the divine consubstantiality of the spark that is in need of being awakened and reintegrated. This gnosis of Gnosticism involves the divine identity of the *knower*, (the Gnostic,) the *known*, (the divine substance of one's transcendent self) and the *means by which* one knows (gnosis as an implicit divine faculty to be awakened and actualised.)' A further point made was a distinction between proto-Gnosticism and pre-Gnosticism. This distinction relates to the question of Gnostic origins. On the one hand the pre-Gnostic is prepared to recognise the existence of themes and motifs, concepts and ideas in the pre-Christian and pre-Gnostic period, which are preparing the way for the development of Gnosticism proper. The proto-Gnostic view however would find the essence of Gnosticism already in the centuries preceding the second century A.D. and also outside of the strictly Christian Gnosticism of the second century. This seems to be a useful distinction, because it sets out clearly the real issue of present discussion and debate. Those scholars who adhere to the proto-Gnostic point of view appeal especially to Iran, the Indo-Iranian world, to Platonism and to Orphism as evidence for their position; those who speak of pre-Gnosticism, on the other hand, emphasise rather Jewish apocalyptic, the Qumran Scrolls, Pharisaism, the atmosphere of crisis in Judaism following upon

[38] See above, n. 30. The proposals for clarification of the definition of terms are given in full by Bianchi, pp. 154 ff.

the fall of Jerusalem in A.D. 70, and also certain currents of Christian thought.

One problem in this connection has already been alluded to in passing, the problem of determining to what extent the same words, the same concepts, even the same statements, preserve their meaning in continuity right through the history of a tradition, and to what extent they may be modified and reinterpreted in course of time. This problem is the more difficult when it is a case not merely of one linguistic tradition, but of several. In a modern language the natural rendering of some term may be the same as that for a term in some other ancient tongue, but there is a danger for us of reading back associations which are not necessarily present in one or other of these ancient languages. Not every reference to 'knowledge' carries with it the special Gnostic significance associated in the Gnostic context with the Greek word *gnosis*, and *gnosis* itself does not in every case refer to 'Gnostic' knowledge. Again, there is a pssage in the Gospel of Truth which employs the Coptic word *mnt-rm-nhēt*.[39] The natural English rendering for this is in some cases 'wisdom', which in turn would suggest the Greek word *sophia*, but in point of fact there is no justification for identifying *mnt-rm-nhēt* and *sophia*. *Sophia* is not given as one of the equivalents for *mnt-rm-nhēt* in Crum's dictionary, nor is it ever used as the equivalent of *sophia* in the Coptic versions of the New Testament. Indeed there are two cases in which *mnt-rm-nhēt* and *sophia*, as a loan word, appear together in the same context, which indicates that they have a difference of meaning.[40] An interpretation based upon the understanding of this word in English could therefore very easily lead to mistranslation and misconception of the passage in the Gospel of Truth.

A further example of the same kind of thing comes with the reinterpretation of passages in a new context. The Epistle to the Hebrews for example quotes the eighth psalm:

> Thou hast made him a little lower than the angels,
> Thou hast crowned him with glory and honour.
>
> (Heb. 2 : 6 ff.)

The author applies this quotation to Jesus, taking 'a little lower' not in the sense of 'on a slightly lower level', but in a temporal

---

[39] Cf. *NTS* 9, (1963), p. 297 f.   [40] Col. 1.9, Eph. 1.8.

sense 'for a short space', which incidentally creates problems for the English translator. If the Gnostics were making such slight modifications and reinterpreting their texts, to what extent are we justified in carrying back the Gnostic interpretation into the original text?

A third example is provided by the motif of the pearl. In the Acts of Thomas we have the well-known Hymn of the Pearl, sometimes called the Hymn of the Soul, which most scholars would agree to interpret as a Gnostic allegory. Admittedly, there are in this hymn obscurities and apparent inconsistencies, which may perhaps suggest the adaptation of older material: is the prince of the story Everyman, sent into the world for a purpose which he fails to accomplish, until he is awakened and recalled to his task? This would be to interpret the pearl in the light of the Gospel parable of the Kingdom of God as a pearl of great price, worthy of the sacrifice of all a man's possessions; and in this case the hymn need not be Gnostic at all. Or is the prince the Saviour, descended to redeem the pearl which is the soul and at first for a time overcome by the deceit of this world, so that he himself has to be awakened—a Salvator salvandus? In some sense he is both, for the Saviour in his descent and ascent, as Bevan long ago observed, duplicates the destiny of the soul. For present purposes, however, these questions are subsidiary to the main point. Jonas[41] quotes a Manichean allegory in which the symbolism is spelt out to the last detail. Moreover the motif is found also in Mandeism, and further back there is the Naassene exegesis of Matt. 7 : 6, according to which this saying refers to 'the pearls of the Unformed One' (identified as 'words and minds and men') 'cast into the formation.' To carry this back to Matthew (Matt. 13 : 45 f.), and interpret the parable of the Pearl of great Price in the light of it, would be an obvious mistake. But what of logion 76 of the Gospel of Thomas, if Thomas is indeed a Gnostic work? Is it to be understood in terms of Matthew or of Gnosticism?

According to the Gospel of Philip (48) a pearl cast in the mud does not lose its value, nor is its worth enhanced by anointing with balsam oil. At an earlier point (Philip 22) the soul is

---

[41] *The Gnostic Religion*, (Boston 1958), pp. 112 ff., esp. p. 126 n.15; also his paper in *The Bible in Modern Scholarship*, ed. J. P. Hyatt, (Nashville 1965), pp. 279 ff.

described as a precious thing which has come to be in a despised body. The similar analogy of gold in mud is mentioned in Irenaeus' account of the system of Ptolemy, and also occurs in Plotinus.[42] The Gospel of Thomas speaks of spirit and flesh in terms of wealth and poverty (log. 29), a saying which readily recalls Paul's reference to 'treasure in earthen vessels' (2 Cor. 4 : 7). Are all these to be grouped together and classified as 'Gnostic'? Or should we not rather recognise the occurrence of a common motif, which may or may not have passed from one tradition to another, and proceed to examine the use that is made of it in different contexts? For it may be not the motif itself but the use that is made of it that is Gnostic. It is pertinent also to note the point made by Jonas,[43] that the Naassene exegesis appeals not to Matt. 13 : 45 f. but to Matt. 7 : 6. In short, it may be a serious error to assume that a motif or symbol always and in every case carries with it the same significance.

One feature of the Messina Colloquium, as already mentioned, was a number of papers in which stress was laid upon the Jewish contribution.[44] Reference has already been made to a number of spheres of influence, Egypt, Persia, Babylonia, Mesopotamia and so on. Of recent years it has been the Jewish element which has perhaps received the greatest emphasis. It was stressed for example by A. D. Nock, while R. M. Grant sought to find the origins of Gnosticism in the disappointed eschatological hopes of Qumran sectarians.[45] G. Quispel has stressed the contribution of heterodox Judaism, Gershom Scholem has noted Gnostic affinities in Jewish mysticism, in the whole tradition reaching right down to the Cabbala.[46] Again, there are certainly affinities with Gnosticism in Jewish apocalyptic, and in much of the writings of Philo, although it

---

[42] Plotinus, *The Enneads*, tr. Stephen McKenna, (²London 1956), p. 60 f. [Enn. I.6.5 ad fin.].

[43] *The Bible in Modern Scholarship*, p. 285 n.9. On the whole question of Christian and Gnostic language see S. Laeuchli, *The Language of Faith*, (Nashville 1962; London 1965).

[44] Cf. above, n. 30.

[45] Grant, *Gnosticism and Early Christianity*, (New York 1959).

[46] Cf. Quispel in *Eranos Jahrb.* XXII, (1953), pp. 195 ff.; *Evang. Theologie*, 1954, pp. 1–11; *The Bible in Modern Scholarship*, pp. 252 ff.; Scholem, *Jewish Gnosticism, Merkabah Mysticism, and Talmudic Tradition*, (New York 1960); *Ursprung und Anfänge der Kabbala*, (Berlin 1962).

should be emphasised that there are also differences. With regard to Scholem's position it must be asked: How far is Jewish mysticism really gnosis? Hans Jonas indeed has spoken of 'the semantic disservice which Scholem did to clarity when he called his Palestinian Hekhaloth mysticism a "gnosis".'[47] Jonas himself writes 'the recent Coptic discoveries are said to underline the share of a heterodox occultist Judaism, though judgement must be reserved pending the translation of the vast body of the material.'[48] In a footnote he adds 'nothing so far presented has to my mind proven the Judaistic thesis', and he continues 'some connection of Gnosticism with the beginnings of the Cabbala has in any case to be assumed, whatever the order of cause and effect. The violently anti-Jewish bias of the more prominent Gnostic systems is by itself not incompatible with Jewish heretical origin at some distance . . . The Jewish strain in Gnosticism is as little the orthodox Jewish as the Babylonian is the orthodox Babylonian, the Iranian the orthodox Iranian, and so on.' Finally, Kurt Rudolph[49] has drawn attention to the anti-Jewish strain in Mandeism—in this respect the Mandeans go with the Gnostics in the stricter sense of the word.

Now there is no question of the place of Jewish elements within the Gnostic systems. There are cases in which the Gnostic myth is little more than a reinterpretation of the Genesis creation story in Gnostic terms. This means that the Gnostics were somehow in contact with circles from which they could obtain the book of Genesis. The question is whether these circles were Jewish or Jewish-Christian,[50] or whether indeed the Gnostics knew no more of Judaism than the book of Genesis itself, whether in fact they were Gentiles who only had a more or less superficial knowledge of Jewish teaching. This is a further indication of the complexity of the problem. Again, in his Messina paper Alexander Böhlig underlined the *Umdeutung* which has taken place in the use of Jewish material in the new Coptic Gnostic texts; in a supplementary note he emphasises

---

[47] *The Bible in Modern Scholarship*, p. 291.

[48] *The Gnostic Religion*, pp. 33 f. Cf. also van Unnik in *Vig Chr.* 15, (1961), pp. 65 ff.

[49] *Die Mandäer*, 1.51 ff.

[50] Cf. J. Daniélou, 'Judéo-christianisme et gnose', in *Aspects du judéo-christianisme*, (Paris 1965); also his *Théologie du judéo-chrstianisme*, (Tournai 1958).

that whatever their original affiliation the men to whom we owe these texts were *Gnostics*, with a different understanding of human existence from that of other religions, a point borne out for example by some statements in the Gospel of Philip (cf. Philip 6 and 46). It is well to heed the warnings which have been uttered against undue reliance upon any particular theory as the complete and sufficient answer to the whole problem of Gnostic origins. 'What we must beware of in these championships of causes is the fallacy of exclusiveness, the lure of fashion, and the hasty identification of any one with the origin of Gnosticism.'[51]

The discussion thus far has inevitably ranged very far afield. It is time now to draw the threads together, and formulate the conclusions which seem to emerge.

1.   The starting point for all investigation must be the 'classical' Gnosticism of the second Christian century and after, for here we have a clearly-defined and manageable group of systems all showing certain common characteristics. It seems desirable to distinguish Gnosticism in this narrower sense from the wider and more nebulous 'Gnosis', although this does not by any means absolve us from the responsibility of investigating the relationship between them, the process of development from one to the other, the channels by which ideas were transmitted, the proximate and ultimate sources from which these ideas were derived.

2.   Gnosticism in this narrower sense must be regarded as a Christian heresy, but this is not the whole story. In the effort to understand the Christian heresy and explain its origins we have to take account of similar phenomena in other areas, religions and systems of thought which show affinities with Gnosticism proper, yet without exact correspondence in point of detail. It is here that the wider conception of Gnosis has its value. Manicheism and Mandeism are obvious cases in point. Related to Gnosticism, they must be reckoned with in any comprehensive study, yet they are sufficiently distinct from the 'classical' Gnosticism to be classified apart. Similarly Marcion shows certain affinities with Gnosticism, but it is open to question whether he should be classified simply as a Gnostic, without qualification. The Hermetica, again, are at least semi-Gnostic, and acquire a new importance from the inclusion of certain Hermetic docu-

[51] Jonas in *The Bible and Modern Scholarship*, p. 284.

ments in the Nag Hammadi library; but here there is no Christian influence. All these may legitimately be grouped under the general heading of Gnosis.

3. In the same way, certain phenomena which appear in the writings of Philo or in the Dead Sea Scrolls, together with the 'Gnostic affinities' which have been found in various parts of the New Testament, may justifiably be included under this general head, although here it may be desirable to use some such term as 'pre-gnosis' to avoid any hasty generalisation or pre-judging of the issue. One problem here is to avoid the reading back into first-century terminology of associations and connotations which that terminology does have in the second century, and at the same time to recognise, already in the first century, the points of growth for second-century theories, or even the emergence in embryonic form of incipient Gnostic systems which only come to full development later.

A useful analogy here is provided by the figure of Wisdom, which in some of our documents is quite definitely and unmistakably hypostatised and personified. In other texts however wisdom is no less clearly just a quality or attribute, and personification does not enter in at all. In a third group, of which the Wisdom of Solomon is an outstanding example, it is a very difficult matter to determine when the reference is to the quality of wisdom and when to the hypostatised semi-divine figure. It may be that the author himself made no conscious distinction between the two, but the fact remains that a change has taken place, and that the Wisdom of Solomon represents a point of transition. It would be a mistake to read back the developed hypostatisation, or the Sophia of the Gnostic documents, into every occurrence of the word in this book, and a still more serious error to carry back these connotations to the earliest documents in which personification has in fact not yet taken place. Yet to understand the whole development we need to keep in mind the final outcome.

4. The problem of Gnostic origins remains a crucial question, and one that is still in debate. In point of fact, it is not one single problem only but several, although not all are of equal significance.

(a) There is for example the problem of the date of the emergence of the Gnostic religion as a recognisable entity, distinct from the vaguely defined trends of thought subsumed under the broader heading of Gnosis. From some points of view this is not a vital question, but for the New Testament scholar and the student of Christian origins it is one of some importance, for it enters into the further question of the relation between Gnosticism and early Christianity. Some scholars confidently speak of Gnostic influence on the early Church, of Gnostic motifs in the New Testament itself; others show a very natural reluctance to admit any such influence. This question calls for more detailed treatment in a later chapter. For the present it may suffice to say that Gnosticism appears to be roughly contemporary with Christianity, or perhaps a little later, and that there are signs of an incipient Gnosticism in the New Testament period; but Gnosis in the broader sense is indisputably older. Hence in any consideration of alleged 'Gnostic influence' on the New Testament we have to ask whether the term 'Gnostic' is being employed *descriptively*, in the sense that the motif in question is Gnostic in the second century, although earlier and in a non-Gnostic context it might not be Gnostic at all; or whether the adjective is used in the sense of *derivation*, to indicate that the term, motif or concept involved was taken over from pre-Christian Gnosis.

(b) A second question is the relation of this pre-Christian Gnosis to the Gnostic Religion and to the second-century sects. To what extent is there continuity of development, and how far can we assume that what is clearly present in Gnosticism but suggested only vaguely, if at all, in Gnosis was already actually current at the earlier stage? The assumption that the full development of later Gnosticism is already present in pre-Christian Gnosis obviously involves a begging of the question, a reading of first-century texts with second-century spectacles, and this amply justifies the reluctance of some scholars, as already mentioned, to admit any widespread 'Gnostic influence' in the formation stages of early Christianity.

(c) A third problem is that of ultimate sources and proximate channels. It is now abundantly clear that the whole background of the late Hellenistic world has to be taken into account, and that attempts to derive the whole movement from one single source far back in the mists of antiquity are one-sided and misleading. To trace the ultimate origins of a particular idea is perfectly legitimate, but it is not the whole story. How, why, where and by whom was this particular idea brought into association with other ideas, often from very different sources, to take its place in the context of the developed Gnostic theories?

There is something undeniably attractive in the suggestion[52] that the unification of the Mediterranean world after the conquests of Alexander, the mingling of the peoples, the growth of cosmopolitanism, the increasing use of Greek as the common language, the emergence of a common philosophy, should all have prompted a drive towards a common religion, a religion for humanity; and the time was to come when Gnosticism and Christianity were competing for this position. But was there a deliberate and conscious effort to *create* such a religion, and if so when and by whom? Or was it a process of gradual development, which reached its culmination in the second Christian century? We do know of one attempt at a synthetic religion, the cult of Serapis, intended by the Ptolemies to form a bond of union for their Greek and Egyptian subjects, but a universal religion would be something on an altogether grander scale. We know also of the syncretism prevalent among the mystery cults, but syncretism is not yet Gnosis.

It would seem more profitable to seek the immediate sources, to try to find the points at which ideas are brought together, or new influences begin to operate. Where, for example, does Greek philosophy come in? Was the trend, in terms of the title of one of Jonas' volumes, 'from mythology to mystical philosophy'? In other words, was the philosophical element a later accretion, showing that Gnosticism like Christianity, and at almost the same period, had to come to terms with contemporary Greek philosophy? In that case, the affinities with Neo-Platonism, and with Middle Platonism earlier, and even with such a writer as Philo, should perhaps be discounted as evidence rather of the influence of philosophy upon Gnosticism than of Gnostic influence upon philosophy.

It is in this context that what Jonas calls 'the Judaistic thesis' calls for serious consideration. There is the undeniable Jewish

---

[52] Cf. Böhlig in *Koptische Kunst*, (Catalogue of the Exhibition of Coptic Art at the Villa Hügel, Essen, May-August 1963), pp. 42 ff., and the supplementary remarks to his Messina paper.

C

element in the Gnostic systems, even though the Jewish materials may be employed in a non-Jewish or even anti-Jewish way. There are the affinities in Philo. There is the prominence as centres of Gnosticism of areas which had a considerable Jewish element in the population, such as the city of Alexandria or the province of Asia Minor. There is the problem, familiar to the New Testament scholar, of determining whether the false teachers opposed in some letter were Jewish or Gnostic: Paul's opponents at Corinth, for example, or the heretics at Colossae; or we may recall the heresies hinted at in the letters of Ignatius. It may be that sometimes we have been too ready to make rigid and clear-cut distinctions where the situation was in fact rather fluid and the lines by no means clearly drawn. Finally, many specific motifs can be traced to a Jewish origin, or shown to have parallels in Jewish sources, and even where some particular motifs derive ultimately from other sources there may be grounds for thinking that it was through the medium of Judaism that they passed into Gnosticism.[53]

These points make up a strong case for the view that Judaism was at the very least an important factor in the development of Gnosticism, but Judaism itself, as we now know, was by no means uniform in the Hellenistic and Roman age. If Gnosticism is the result of an amalgamation of paganism and Christianity, the natural place to look for Jewish anticipations, a pre-Christian Jewish Gnosticism, would be the Diaspora; but there are Jewish elements in Gnosticism which are not to be found in the voluminous pages of Philo, although Alexandria was later to become one of the chief centres of Gnosticism. Again, some of the closest parallels to the Gospel of Thomas and the Gospel of Philip occur in Rabbinic sources, and the same holds for some of the material adduced by Böhlig in his Messina paper.[54] Does this mean that these elements are older, dating back before the split of Church and Synagogue, or are they evidence of a prolonged contact well into the second century, even after the revolt under Hadrian?

Finally, there are the parallels to which Scholem has drawn attention between Gnosticism and Jewish mysticism. Here it

[53] Cf. Rudolph, *Wiss. Zeitschr. Jena*, pp. 89 ff.

[54] *Der jüdische und judenchristliche Hintergrund in gnostischen Texten von Nag Hammadi.*

must be emphasised once again that while mysticism may be classed as Gnosis it is not necessarily Gnosticism. As Jonas puts it,[55] 'A Gnosticism without a fallen god, without benighted creator and sinister creation, without alien soul, cosmic captivity and acosmic salvation, without the self-redeeming of the Deity —in short: a Gnosis without divine tragedy will not meet specifications'. In contrast, the Jewish mystics with whom Scholem is concerned, for all their esotericism and 'gnosticising' tendencies, are in the last resort monotheistic and essentially orthodox, Jews rather than Gnostics, and the same must also be said of the Qumran sect. Sectarianism and heterodoxy do not necessarily amount to Gnosticism, although they may contribute to it and prepare the way.

R. M. Grant has traced the origins of Gnosticism to the disappointed eschatological hopes of Qumran sectarians,[56] which may be correct up to a point. I should prefer to say that *some* Gnostics may have formerly been Qumran sectarians, as others may have been former proselytes, both reacting in utter revulsion to the Fall of Jerusalem and the collapse of their hopes and expectations, and therefore degrading the God of Israel to the status of an inferior Demiurge. Others again might have been Christians: Mlle Pétrement has shown that some elements are explicable in terms of development within the Church, reflecting the conflict of Church and Synagogue.[57] Others might have been pagans, mocking at the Jews from whom they derived so much. But here we are in the realm of speculation. All we can say is that each is possible, but that probably none of them contains the whole story.

Little or nothing has yet been said in this chapter of the theory of the Gnostic Redeemer-myth, and this of set purpose. In the first place, this theory is no longer so central to the modern debate as it formerly was, and secondly Walter Schmithals, who has presented the fullest and most complete recent discussion, betrays its weakness when he writes that it is actually the result of a combination of two disparate myths; for he does not pause to ask when and by whom the combination was

[55] *The Bible in Modern Scholarship*, p. 293.

[56] *Gnosticism and Early Christianity*, (New York 1959).

[57] In her Messina paper; cf. more generally *Rev. de Métaphysique et de Morale* 65, (1960), pp. 385 ff.

effected. There were admittedly, in the ancient world, saviour-gods in abundance; Osiris is but one example. There were also myths, in various forms, of a Primal Man. But the full development of the theory in which the Heavenly Man descends into the realm of matter to be imprisoned there, and to leave behind on his deliverance something of himself which has to be recovered—this comes very much later as a synthesis of older ideas, probably incorporating also something of the *soma-sema* conception of the body as the tomb of the soul. As Carsten Colpe has put it,[58] we can document from known systems all the ideas embodied in the theory; nor is it simply to be dismissed as a modern mosaic constructed from materials of diverse origin, which largely coincides with the Manichean system. The real flaw is the idea that the myth of the Gnostic Redeemer originated at some time in dim antiquity, somewhere in the remoter East (vaguely conceived as 'Iran'), and then passed across the world and down the centuries, leaving behind scattered fragments in different circles of tradition until at last it was reconstituted as a unity in Manicheism and finally disintegrated into its several components in Mandeism. Rather should we conclude, with H. M. Schenke,[59] that there was no Redeemer-myth in the full sense before Manicheism. It is the climax and the culmination of the long process of development, not its original starting-point. Schenke's demonstration that the Gnostic Anthropos-doctrine owes its origin to speculation on Genesis 1.26 f. provides further confirmation of the importance of the Jewish element in the development of Gnosticism.

It is no exaggeration to say that Nag Hammadi marks the beginning of a new era in the study of Gnosticism.[60] Twenty years ago our resources consisted entirely of the Christian refutations written by the early Fathers, and of such Gnostic material as they chose to quote, together with the merest handful of original Gnostic documents, and these of late date, preserved in Coptic. Even ten years ago the three Gnostic texts

[58] Schmithals, *Die Gnosis in Korinth*, (Göttingen 1956), p. 82; Colpe, *Die religionsgeschichtliche Schule*, (Göttingen 1961), p. 191.

[59] *Der Gott 'Mensch' in der Gnosis*, (Göttingen 1962), p. 148.

[60] For the library in general cf. Doresse, *The Secret Books of the Egyptian Gnostics*, (ET: London 1960). Bibliography to 1963 by S. Giversen, *Studia Theologica* 17, (1963), pp. 139 ff.

in the Berlin Coptic papyrus had not yet been published, although their existence and their contents had been known for more than half a century; but that is another story.[61] Now we have from Nag Hammadi something like 1000 pages of Coptic text, much of it in a good state of preservation—more than forty documents hitherto quite unknown, to make no mention of the duplicates of texts in the Berlin Codex or of documents in the Nag Hammadi collection itself. So far a dozen have been edited and published, including three versions of the Apocryphon of John, already known from the Berlin text. If on the one hand progress appears disappointingly slow, there is this to be said on the other side: first that there were legal difficulties to be surmounted before publication could begin, not to speak of problems arising out of the political situation, and secondly that the preparation of a satisfactory edition requires time, for the number of people competent to undertake such a task is by no means large. Moreover most of us will be grateful for some interval between one document and the next—the prospect of the release of 1000 pages of Coptic text at one fell swoop is, to say the least, somewhat daunting for anyone who may have to deal with them!

As already noted, the texts so far published led Nock to express the opinion that they confirm the traditional view of Gnosticism as a Christian heresy. This is not in the least surprising, since these texts in fact belong to the Christian era and derive from the second century or later. Some of them indeed fit neatly into the accounts of the Gnostic systems provided by Irenaeus. It remains to be seen whether all the remaining texts are of the same character, or whether some of them may admit of the detection of an older *Grundschrift*. As it happens, the editor of one of the latest volumes claims to have found a pre-Christian document among his texts,[62] and there are cases in which it has been maintained that we can see the hand of a Christian redactor.[63] Here much has still to be done, first in the way of publication, then in the study and comparison and analysis of

---

[61] See W. C. Till, *Die gnostischen Schriften des koptischen Papyrus Berolinensis 8502* (*TU* 60, Berlin 1955).

[62] Böhlig, *Koptisch-gnostische Apokalypsen aus Codex V von Nag Hammadi*, (Halle-Wittenberg 1963); see below on the Apocalypse of Adam.

[63] See below on the Apocryphon of John and the Sophia Jesu Christi.

the texts. Even if they do not supply the answer to our questions about Gnostic origins, these texts still have their value, for they will enable us to study the development of Gnostic ideas, the elaboration of Gnostic documents, the ways in which themes and concepts were adopted and adapted, possibly even to establish the course of the development in chronological sequence. Above all they will give us an insight into the meaning which Gnosticism possessed for the Gnostic. Reference has already been made to Bigg's disparaging comment, with which most of those who have concerned themselves with the subject must at some time have felt themselves in agreement. Yet this queer farrago of nonsense does have a meaning, when the clues are known, and there are passages of genuine religious feeling in such documents as the Gospel of Truth or the Gospel of Philip.

To sum up, the broad picture is fairly clear, particularly where we are concerned with the developed Gnosticism of the second century and later, but there are still many gaps in our knowledge: the precise relationship of different groups, the ways in which they influenced one another, the sources upon which they drew. In the earliest stages in particular much is still uncertain. We can indeed speak of an incipient Gnosticism in the New Testament period, but how much of the developed later Gnosticism was already present at any given stage is still obscure. It has been said that we can see two attitudes in the New Testament writings, one of tolerance in a period of mutual interpenetration, and one of rejection and resistance,[64] and this may probably be considered as broadly accurate. It is not uncommon for 'heretic' and 'orthodox' to live in peaceful co-existence for a period before the lines of division become distinct, or for the men of one generation to tolerate with equanimity ideas which a later age would denounce. This means that in our investigations we must constantly pay heed to accurate definition, and ask whether a word or concept in any given case must necessarily carry the associations which it has in a different context of ideas. Sometimes, again, we need to consider whether we are in fact asking the proper questions, or drawing the correct conclusions from our data. And when it comes to assessing the possibility of influence from one source or another due attention must be given to considerations or chronology.

[64] Haenchen in *RGG*³ II, col. 1652.

II

'Gnosticism' in the New Testament

IN the light of the discussion in the previous chapter, the above title must appear to be erroneous. If Gnosticism is defined as the Christian heresy of the second century, then obviously there can be no such thing as Gnosticism in the New Testament, and to think in these terms is to run the risk of interpreting first-century documents in the light of second-century ideas. The title has however been deliberately chosen, and for various reasons.

In the first place, the preceding discussion has explicitly recognised (a) that Gnosis in the broader sense is pre-Christian, and may therefore have exercised some influence on the New Testament; and (b) that there are indications of an incipient Gnosticism, in the narrower sense of that term, within the New Testament period. The aim of this chapter is to explore this question in greater detail, to make some attempt to define and delimit the areas of 'gnostic' influence, in the wider sense of the term, in the New Testament literature, and to trace so far as possible the emergence and, it may be, the development of this incipient Gnosticism. Secondly, the alternative title 'Gnosticism *and* the New Testament' would also be misleading, since it could cover not only the subject of the present chapter but also that of the chapter following. In examining the relationship between Gnosticism and the New Testament we have to take account not only of the 'gnostic motifs' and 'gnostic influences' which scholars have claimed to find in the New Testament, but also of the clear and indisputable use that was made by the Gnostics of the New Testament itself. The relationship in fact is not a simple one, with the debt always and wholly on the side of the New Testament and of Christianity. Whatever the date of the emergence of Gnosticism as a fully-developed religion in its own right, we have to think rather of a period of mutual inter-pretation in which Christianity was confronted first by the older vaguely-defined Gnosis, and later by the initial stirrings of an incipient Gnosticism, and in which each in some measure re-acted to and was influenced by the other.

At this stage the situation is still fluid, the lines of division not yet clearly drawn. As has already been said, it is by no means uncommon for 'heretic' and 'orthodox' to live in peaceful co-existence for a period, for the men of one generation to tolerate with equanimity ideas and conceptions, theories and doctrines, which a later generation will denounce as heretical. It is only in the light of subsequent developments that we can determine which was to become the 'orthodox' position and which the 'heretical'. We have therefore to guard against the danger of judging by the standards of a later age, of transferring the clear distinctions of a later period back into a situation in which the final cleavage had not yet taken place and the full implications of a particular theory had not yet been realised. This, it need hardly be said, only adds to the delicacy and complexity of our task.

A further problem concerns the method of approach. One possible line of procedure would be to ransack the commen-taries and ancillary literature and cull from them every passage, ever motif, every term which has at any time been classified as 'Gnostic'. We should then have to examine each in turn, to determine whether it is in fact Gnostic, and in what sense: whether it derives from the vaguer pre-Christian Gnosis, or is only Gnostic in the narrower sense because it appears in the theories of the second-century sects. In the former case we should have to enquire whether it is a specifically gnostic influence upon Christianity, or derives from some other move-ment, be it some school of Greek philosophy, or Jewish apo-calyptic, or some other field of ancient thought. In the latter case it is open to question whether in the New Testament such a motif should be classed as 'Gnostic' at all, or whether we should not think in terms of Gnostic borrowing and adaptation from the New Testament itself. A third possibility of course is that of parallel development, ideas and concepts of a similar character being utilised in the same way in Christianity and in Gnosis, or later in Gnosticism proper. And a fourth possibility is that ideas from the vaguer Gnosis may have been taken over and adapted to their own purposes by the New Testament writers, and then

later adopted from Christianity by the Gnostics, who re-interpreted them in the light of their own ideas.

Such theoretical possibilities could no doubt be multiplied,
and only serve to increase the complexity of the problem. How
are we to distinguish one kind of motif from another, the
'parallel developments' from those derived by Gnosticism and
Christianity alike from Platonism or Stoicism or Judaism? Nor
are our difficulties lightened by the fact that, when we try to
push back, the vague pre-Christian Gnosis tends to become even
vaguer and more nebulous, indeed to evaporate until it is little
more than an attitude of mind which comes to expression in the
documents of various schools of thought. It is this that prompts
the outright denial of the very existence of a 'pre-Christian
Gnosticism' by such writers as Alan Richardson. But it must be
remembered that we are probing back in search of the first
tentative beginnings of a movement which came to full flower
only later.

Desirable as it might be to have this line of approach followed
up, and the whole range of material brought under scrutiny,
the weaknesses and disadvantages are obvious. In the first place,
there is the sheer amount of labour involved, not to mention
problems of space and documentation, or of the avoidance of
duplication. Nor is it even certain that the results would be
commensurate. And secondly the problem would be complicated by the need to investigate at every turn the precise
conception of Gnosis or of Gnosticism held by the modern
scholars concerned.

The present chapter accordingly proposes something a great
deal less ambitious: first, an attempt to clarify the situation
within the New Testament itself, to identify those areas in
which an incipient Gnosticism may with some confidence be
detected in the background, and distinguish them on the one
hand from those which present no such phenomena, and on the
other from those where the Gnostic element or Gnostic influence
is either hypothetical or debated; and secondly, an examination
of some of the motifs which have been claimed as Gnostic,
bearing in mind the various possibilities outlined above, with a
view to their classification so far as may be possible under the
proper heads.

By way of further introduction, reference may be made to

two contrasting examples of the modern approach. Bultmann in his *Theology* has a whole section under the heading 'Gnostic Motifs',[1] in which he affirms that Paul's anthropological concepts had already been formed under the influence of Gnosticism, and that Paul himself 'regards the Gnostic terminology as the appropriate form of expression for the Christian understanding of existence.' In his little book *Primitive Christianity in its Contemporary Setting*[2] he lists a number of terms which, he affirms, are mythological and derived from Gnosticism. Alan Richardson on the other hand, in words already quoted,[3] says 'The objection to speaking of Gnosticism in the first century A.D. is that we are in danger of hypostatising certain rather ill-defined tendencies of thought and then speaking as if there were a religion or religious philosophy, called Gnosticism, which could be contrasted with Judaism or Christianity. There was, of course, no such thing.' Further on he says 'when scholars like Bultmann describe a Gnostic doctrine they take their first-century "evidence" from the New Testament itself. But this is a question-begging proceeding, since the New Testament is susceptible of a very different interpretation.' And finally, 'those scholars who readily find Gnostic influences at work in the New Testament argue that the beginnings of this type of thought must have been fairly well defined in the first century; they then set out to look for evidences of it in the New Testament, and are then in peril of interpreting the earlier by means of the later writings.'

Here then we have a direct and head-on collision, but it should be observed that this conflict is due at least in part to difference of definition. Richardson on the one hand is working with the traditional definition, on which obviously there can be no talk of Gnosticism in the New Testament, except in such parts as we may see fit to date in the second century. The movement is in one direction only, from the first century to the second, from the New Testament to Gnosticism; and the only question concerns the use that was made by the Gnostics of the New Testament documents. Now so long as we confine our attention to the Christian sphere, within the limits of the history

[1] *Theology of the NT*, i, (ET: London 1952), pp. 164 ff.
[2] *Primitive Christianity*, (ET: London 1956), p. 190.
[3] *Introduction to the Theology of the NT*, (London 1958), pp. 41 ff.

of Christian doctrine, this position is both tenable and valid; but it leaves two questions outstanding: first, how are we to account for this curious second-century deviation? Was it purely a development *within* Christianity, or were extraneous factors at work? In the latter case, what other factors were in fact influential? And secondly, how are we to account for elements in the New Testament itself, and in contemporary or even earlier documents, which seem to bear a distinct resemblance to certain aspects of the second-century Gnosticism?

Bultmann on the other hand is working with the wider definition. As it happens, both his translators in the English editions of the books cited make use of the English word 'Gnosticism', but this with the adjective 'Gnostic' is to say the least misleading; for Bultmann himself consistently speaks of *die Gnosis*.[4] It is for this reason that an attempt was made above to reach a clearer definition by distinguishing between Gnosis in the wider sense and Gnosticism proper. We have to recognise the affinities, even the anticipations, which are undoubtedly present, or we cannot fully understand the development of the Christian heresy. On the other hand, Richardson's criticisms present a necessary warning, which must be borne in mind: (a) we probably should not claim as 'Gnostic influence' those elements in the New Testament which are capable of another interpretation *as well as the Gnostic*. Here the issue should rather be left open. And (b) we must constantly beware of the danger of reading back.

Taking the field of Gnostic studies as a whole, we can distinguish three fairly well defined and clear-cut stages, two of them sufficiently well documented for us to speak with some confidence. These are the second and third, the traditional Gnosticism of the second century and later, and the further developments in Manicheism and Mandeism. The first stage is the period of the New Testament itself, and it is here that the burning questions arise. For that very reason it is incumbent upon us to move with caution. Nothing is easier than to formulate an *Arbeitshypothese*, that because some term or concept is Gnostic at the second stage it may in the New Testament be a case of influence from Gnosis; then to apply the theory to the

---

[4] The same holds at some points in W. G. Kümmel's *Introduction to the NT*, (ET: London 1966).

New Testament occurrences, ignoring the possible alternatives and explaining away the inconvenient evidence; and so to emerge with the 'proof' of 'Gnostic influence'. It is much more difficult to take all the evidence into account, to discriminate between the various possibilities, to distinguish those cases in which the influence of Gnosis must be considered certain, because there is no alternative explanation, from those in which such an influence is merely possible. Our results in the latter case may be much less conclusive, our solutions much less neat and tidy, but it is only by following this more difficult procedure that we can achieve any real and lasting progress.

A convenient starting-point for our investigation is provided by Ernst Haenchen's article in *Die Religion in Geschichte und Gegenwart*,[5] in which he distinguishes two stages in the relationship between New Testament Christianity and Gnosis, using the latter term, of course, in the wider sense. In the first, 'gnostic' ideas and concepts are employed, but any further penetration of Gnosis is resisted, whereas in the second Gnosis is treated simply as false doctrine, and any *Auseinandersetzung* with it is forbidden. These two periods incidentally overlap to some extent in time. This seems to point in the right direction, although there are places at which we may feel called upon to differ from Haenchen's assessment. For example, it is at least open to question whether Paul's opponents in Corinth rejected a future resurrection of the body in favour of a present one in the Spirit; that is, whether the heresy of 2 Tim. 2.18, that the resurrection has already passed, was already current in Corinth in Paul's life-time. Again, it may well be that the Pastorals are directed against Gnosticism, but does this justify the assumption that 1 Tim. 5.23 'hints at a Gnostic prohibition of wine'? Are all forms of asceticism, or abstinence of any kind, to be claimed without more ado as Gnostic, or are there other possibilities? Thirdly, it is again open to question whether we should see a Christianisation of Gnostic material in the contrast of νήπιοι and τέλειοι at Heb. 5.14, or in the identification at Heb. 10.20 of the veil with the flesh of Jesus. The contrast certainly fits the pattern of later Gnostic thinking, but surely it is one that would readily come to mind, without the necessity of any

[5] *RGG*[3] II, cols. 1652 ff.

'Gnostic' influence. The two references listed by Bauer[6] from Philo (*Leg. all.* 1.94; *De sobr.* 9) do not demand a Gnostic interpretation, and even if Philo is to be assigned to the realm of Gnosis in the wider sense, what of Polybius?

> For while they (the Aetolians) had hoped to find a helpless infant in Philip (παίδιον νήπιον), owing to his tender years and inexperience, they really found him to be a grown-up man (τέλειος ἀνήρ), both in his projects and in his performances.
> (Polyb. 5.29.2, tr. W. R. Paton in Loeb Classical Library)

To reckon Polybius as Gnostic would be *Pangnostizismus* indeed!

This contrast, then, should rather be regarded as a very natural metaphor which *in a Gnostic context* could take on a technical sense, but which is not for that reason to be claimed as Gnostic at every occurrence.[7] The case of the veil is more difficult, and should perhaps be left an open question. On the one hand, the idea of a barrier between the higher and the lower realms does play a part in the later Gnostic systems, and in the Gospel of Philip this barrier is symbolised by the veil (76, 125; cf. *SJC* 118.7 ff.); but one of the passages in Philip (125) presents a combination of motifs which appear in Hebrews itself and in the Synoptic Passion Story, so that some influence *from Hebrews* upon Gnostic thinking is not to be ruled out. On the other hand the motif of the Celestial Veil itself goes back to late Jewish speculation,[8] and may have passed directly into Gnosticism from there. Indeed it may already have figured in the older and vaguer Gnosis, in which case only the motif of the *rending* of the veil could be claimed as Christian influence.

There is also, however, a problem of exegesis here.[9] It is certainly natural to take the final words Τοῦτ' ἐστιν τῆς

---

[6] *Wörterbuch*, (⁴Berlin 1952), col. 1470; cf. also col. 975 and note Matt. 11.25.

[7] Cf. also Bertram in Kittel, *TWB*, iv, pp. 913 ff.; P. J. du Plessis, *ΤΕΛΕΙΟΣ. The Idea of Perfection in the NT*, (Kampen n.d.).

[8] Cf. A. Adam, *Die Psalmen des Thomas* . . . , (Beiheft 24 zur *ZNW*, Berlin 1959), p. 35 n.15, and more fully G. W. MacRae, (Cambridge thesis 1966).

[9] Michel [*Hebräerbrief*, (Göttingen 1966), p. 345 n. 2] quotes Käsemann as seeing here a connection with Gnostic mythology; but cf. also the commentaries of Westcott, (1909), Spicq, (1952), Héring, (1954), Montefiore, (1964) for other views.

σαρκὸς αὐτοῦ as standing in apposition to, and explanatory of, the preceding τοῦ καταπετάσματος, which produces the identification mentioned above. If the flesh is the barrier which separates man from God, we are certainly in the realm of 'Gnostic' ideas. This interpretation is however widely recognised to be difficult, on various grounds. One alternative, not generally favoured, is the deletion of the final words as a gloss; another, frequently adopted, is to take them as explanatory not of the veil but of the way. Yet even if we accept the identification it is by no means certain that we have to do with Gnosticism, or even with Gnosis in the wider sense. Moffatt[10] writes 'instead of saying that (Jesus') sacrificial death meant the rending of the veil (like the author of Mark 15.38), *i.e. the supersession of the Old Testament barriers between God and man,* he allegorises the veil here as the flesh of Christ; this had to be rent before the blood could be shed, which enabled him to enter and open God's presence for the people. It is a daring, poetical touch, and the parallelism is not to be prosaically pressed into any suggestion that the human nature in Jesus hid God from men' (italics mine). Such allegorisation is by no means alien to the author's mind, as can be seen from numerous other examples in the Epistle. Here then no assumption of Gnostic influence is necessary, but it can readily be seen how a Gnostic later could re-interpret the passage in the sense not of the Old Testament barriers of sin and the law but in that of the barrier between the realms of flesh and spirit. The motif of the veil thus provides an excellent example of the way in which Gnostic thinking developed, but it is by no means certain that we ought to think of Gnostic influence upon the author of Hebrews. There are other possibilities which must also be considered.

With the motif of the veil Haenchen links that of the 'middle wall of partition' in Eph. 2.14, on which he has earlier said 'The Gnostic idea of the dividing wall which hinders the ascent of the soul to the Pleroma becomes at 2.14–16 the μεσότοιχον between Jews and Gentiles, removed by Christ.' Here again the commentaries are at variance. English-speaking commentators generally cite the wall in the Temple at Jerusalem, between the Court of the Gentiles and the inner precincts, and the warning inscriptions which have been discovered. Not so the German

[10] *Hebrews*, (*I.C.C.*, Edinburgh 1924), p. 143.

scholar—Dibelius[11] asks if the Ephesians would have understood the reference, and claims that this conception belongs to
the Gnostic world of thought: the wall is the division between
man and God, the firmament that separates this world from the
heavenly realm above. But the earliest parallel he quotes is from
Ignatius, and the closest is Mandean. Schlier,[12] as it happens,
quotes a series of passages from Qumran and Jewish Apocalyptic—but it is surely legitimate to ask if the Ephesians would have
understood these references! In point of fact, a preacher in
search of a vivid illustration for the reconciliation of Jew and
Gentile could hardly have found one better, and Paul who had
lived in Jerusalem might well have used it often enough in
Ephesus for the readers to recognise it, or for some disciple to
recall it as one of the hall-marks of Paul's preaching. This is not
to deny the possibility that the Gnostic conception of the
dividing wall may have developed from other roots, or that the
germ of the idea may already have been in existence in the time
of Paul—it is simply to question the assumption that the Gnostic
conception and this alone provides us with the clue to the
meaning of this passage in Ephesians. The problem is much
more complex. We have in fact a number of distinct but similar
ideas which are certainly pre-Christian, and indeed go back to
various forms of primitive cosmology, but which could readily
be combined. One form of the combination appears in the
Gnostic theory, but how far this combination had taken place
when Ephesians was written, and whether it had any influence
upon the author, is very much open to question.

Haenchen very properly deals with the New Testament documents in roughly chronological order, beginning with Paul and
passing in turn to the Synoptics, John, Acts, the deutero-
Paulines and the later books. For present purposes however it
would seem more appropriate to begin where the situation is
fairly clear, to work out, as it were, from the well-lit area
immediately beneath the spot-light, recognising that as we move
outward the light grows progressively weaker until it merges
completely into the darkness. Correspondingly it becomes more
and more difficult to see distinctly and clearly as we progress.

Working back from the well-defined systems of the second

[11] *Hbuch zum NT* 12, (Tübingen 1953), p. 69.
[12] *Epheserbrief*, ad loc.

century, we have in the first instance the fairly clear incipient Gnosticism combatted in 1 John. The two key-notes here are the Docetic Christology, denying that Jesus is come in the flesh (4.2: every spirit which confesses that Jesus Christ has come in the flesh is of God, and every spirit which does not confess Jesus is not of God), perhaps also denying the crucifixion (5.6: not with water only but with the water and the blood), and a certain indifference to morality in matters of conduct. It is not really possible to identify this heresy with any known Gnostic group, but it is close to the teaching of Cerinthus so far as we know it. In the light of the significance later given by the Gnostics to the chrism, as for example in the Gospel of Truth and the Gospel of Philip, it is probable that we should see a polemic edge to the two references in this letter (2.20,27), which contain the only three occurrences of the word in the New Testament.[13] In this case the author would be turning the vocabulary of his opponents against them. On the other hand, the evidence for anointing with oil in other contexts (e.g. James 5.14) makes it impossible to regard this as a *primary* argument here, and further we must beware of assuming that the developed Gnostic theory of a later period is already present.[14]

Jude likewise denounces 'ungodly persons who pervert the grace of our God into licentiousness and deny our only Master and Lord, Jesus Christ.' Nothing very specific is said about the nature of their teaching, but a later reference to Balaam's error might perhaps be linked with the references in Revelation (2.14) to Balaam 'who taught Balak to put a stumbling-block before the sons of Israel, that they might eat food sacrificed to idols and practise immorality.' Balaam however is only one of three Old Testament figures mentioned in Jude 11, and may therefore be merely a typical example; nor are idolatry and immorality in themselves adequate criteria for the identification of Gnostics, otherwise we should have to regard Gnosticism as very much older and more widely spread than we have any reason to believe. The reference to Balaam in 2 Peter 2.15

[13] Cf. Dodd, *The Johannine Epistles*, (London 1946), pp. 58 ff.; Schnackenburg, *Die Johannesbriefe*, (Freiburg 1963), 152 f.

[14] On the use of chrismation in the early Church cf. G. W. H. Lampe, *The Seal of the Spirit*, (London 1951); L. L. Mitchell, *Baptismal Anointing*, (London 1966).

would lend itself more readily to association with the passage in Revelation, but the dependence of 2 Peter on Jude, now widely recognised, must give us pause; the author may have had reasons of his own for selecting only one of the three Old Testament figures for mention. Finally, the Nicolaitans who appear in the same context in Revelation may have stood under the same condemnation; but their relation on the one hand to the Nicolaus of Acts 6.5 and on the other to the later sect of the name is by no means clear.

The Pastoral Epistles provide the famous admonition 'avoid the godless chatter and contradictions of what is falsely called knowledge' (1 Tim. 6.20), which supplied Irenaeus with his term—and is at the bottom of our whole problem! Here controversy with the false teachers is discouraged, as leading only to useless strife and controversy, and certainly there are elements which suggest a Gnostic character for the opposition (e.g. 2 Tim. 2.18—the resurrection past already; possibly also a Docetic Christology, cf. 2 Tim. 2.8; 1 Tim. 2.5 ff., 3.16); but sometimes a specifically *Gnostic* character has to be inferred, and is not necessary stated—are the 'myths and genealogies' of 1 Tim. 1.4 (cf. Titus 3.9) necessarily to be identified, in Haenchen's words, with 'Gnostic sequences of the powers in the Pleroma, in the manner of Irenaeus *haer.* I.30,5'? The description in 1 Tim. 4.3 of people who forbid marriage and enjoin abstinence from certain foods would fit some Gnostics; but were these Gnostics the only people to practise such asceticism? The demand for celibacy as a pre-requisite for baptism in the early Syrian Church[15] may be the result of Gnostic influence, and such later documents as the Acts of Thomas would certainly appear to have been at least influenced by Gnosticism, but what of an earlier period? In Pythagoreanism celibacy, if not required, was at least highly esteemed; some Essenes at any rate were celibate, and Matthew Black has traced this ascetic element in Essenism to the ancient Israelite institution of the Nazirate.[16] Moreover a

---

[15] A. Vööbus, *Celibacy. A Requirement for Admission to Baptism in the Early Church*, (Stockholm 1951). A. F. J. Klijn, *The Acts of Thomas*, (Leiden 1962), pp. 192 ff., doubts Vööbus' view that a promise of virginity was required. Cf. more generally H. Chadwick, art. Enkrateia in *RAC* 5, (1962), cols. 343 ff.; F. Bolgiani, 'La tradizione eresiologica sull' encratismo', *Atti Acad. Torino* 96, (1962), pp. 1–128.

[16] *The Scrolls and Christian Origins*, (London 1961), pp. 27 ff.

D

passage quoted by Black from Schürer[17] suggests the advisability of caution here: 'Since the act of marriage as such made an individual unclean and necessitated a Levitical bath of purification, the effort to attain to the highest degree of purity might well lead to the entire repudiation of marriage.' It is not difficult to believe that such conceptions of purity and holiness were not confined to the Jews alone, but may have been widely current. Here again, then, we have something which may be Gnostic *in a Gnostic context*, but is not necessarily to be employed as a primary criterion for the detection of Gnostic influence.

At this point we seem to be near the border-line where things become obscure and hard to identify with precision. All the documents so far mentioned contain attacks on false teaching, but the precise nature of the heresy is nearly always difficult to grasp. 1 John perhaps presents the clearest picture, but even here we are not told much that we should like to know. It is the cumulative effect of a number of features shared with the later Gnostics by the opponents attacked in these documents which makes us think of an incipient Gnosticism as the heresy in view. But there is nothing, in the first place, to suggest that this incipient Gnosticism had as yet advanced very far in the direction of later developments; nor in the second place are we given any clear indication as to whether it was the result of the meeting of Christianity with something from outside, already more or less fully developed, or whether we have to do only with a more or less sporadic outbreak of false teaching in different areas, but within Christianity itself.

A further point to be noted is that in Titus 1.14 the 'myths' are described as Jewish, and are linked with 'the commands of men who overturn the truth.' The same letter earlier speaks of insubordinate men, empty talkers and deceivers, *especially the circumcision party*' (1.10). According to 1 Tim. 1.7, the opponents wish to be 'teachers of the law'. There was therefore, to say the least, a considerable Jewish element in the false teaching, which provides additional confirmation of what has already been said about the significance of the Jewish contribution to the development of Gnosticism. As will appear later, there are passages in other documents where it is sometimes extremely difficult to say

---

[17] *History of the Jewish People*, II.ii, (ET: Edinburgh 1885), p. 211 [Black, p. 29 n. 4].

whether the false teaching was Jewish or Gnostic, the Colossian heresy providing a good example. If we could assume that Paul's opponents were always of the same uniform character, and that the Pastoral Epistles and Colossians are authentic Pauline letters, we could then claim that Paul throughout was contending against Jewish Gnostics or Gnosticising Jewish Christians, and this in turn would involve pushing back the origins of Gnosticism to an earlier period. It is obvious, however, that this involves a number of assumptions which are at least doubtful, and which many scholars would regard as without real foundation. The evidence seems rather to suggest a gradual development. In Galatians we seem to have to do with Judaisers who may have made room in their theories for some of the speculations which later came to be known as Gnostic.[18] In the Colossian heresy this 'Gnostic colouring' is more prominent, in the Pastorals perhaps more prominent still; but even here, as Kelly puts it,[19] it is 'something much more elementary' than the developed Gnostic systems of the second century.

One obvious problem is that of dating, another that of authenticity; and in neither case can it be claimed that scholars generally are in complete agreement.[20] There may be a wide consensus of opinion that the Pastorals are post-Pauline, but there are nonetheless still some who would maintain their authenticity, and that on grounds which are not simply to be dismissed without further ado. Now if these documents are dated late, somewhere into the early second century, we can reasonably contemplate the possibility of Gnostic influence on the false teaching they attack; but we cannot claim them as valid evidence for an earlier period. There is too an obvious danger of arguing in a circle here, by using the 'Gnostic' element to prove the Pastorals late, and then using the Pastorals as evidence for Gnosticism in the New Testament. It is however worthy of note that those scholars who claim the existence of a pre-Christian

[18] I cannot accept the theory advanced by Schmithals, *Paulus und die Gnostiker*, (Hamburg-Bergstedt 1965), pp. 9 ff. Cf. my paper at the Oxford NT Congress 1965 [in the press], and see Kümmel, *Introd. to the NT*, (ET: London 1965), pp. 194 f.

[19] J. N. D. Kelly, *The Pastoral Epistles*, (London 1963), p. 12.

[20] Contrast, for example, Kelly's commentary and that of C. K. Barrett, (Oxford 1963).

Gnosticism have not to my knowledge attempted to date the Pastorals early and use them as evidence for Paul's own lifetime. Where so much is uncertain, the safest procedure is one of cautious reserve. Perhaps all we can say is that these documents provide evidence (a) for certain trends in a Gnostic direction, and (b) for a considerable Jewish element in this development. 1 John seems to indicate that the process was fairly well advanced, though not yet fully developed, by the end of the first century. How much further back we can trace its origins is still obscure.

In the Synoptics Haenchen finds but one echo, the famous 'Johannine thunderbolt' in Matt. 11.27 and its Lucan parallel. This is in striking contrast with Leisegang's assertion[21] that 'the Christian Gospels, which appeared in the Hellenistic world in the Greek language, were all more or less full of or pervaded by Gnostic motifs'. Unfortunately Leisegang provides neither examples nor documentation, so that it is not clear which Gospels he means. Possibly he actually had only John in mind, since the Synoptic passages listed in his index all appear to be passages re-interpreted by the Gnostics later for their own purposes. A further point to be noted here is the curious fact that Matt. 11.27 is not cited in the Gospel of Thomas, although this document does contain a version of the verses immediately following (log. 90). What is beyond question is that the Synoptic Gospels later provided the material for much Gnostic speculation, and also that Thomas at times shows a special affinity with Luke; but this of course does not make the Synoptics themselves 'Gnostic', or prove that they were subject to Gnostic influence.

A recent study of Luke's purpose in writing takes up another aspect. Starting from the fact that earlier scholars have called attention to items in Luke and Acts which 'seem to imply Luke's awareness of and response to a Gnostic problem', Charles H. Talbert[22] argues that these two works were written 'for the express purpose of serving as a defense against Gnosticism.' The main arguments rest upon the emphasis placed by Luke on the authenticity of the apostolic witness, the legitimacy of the Church's interpretation of Scripture, and the succession of tradition—the three bulwarks of the later Church's defence

---

[21] H. Leisegang, *Die Gnosis*, (Stuttgart 1955), pp. 2 f.

[22] *Luke and the Gnostics*, (Nashville 1966); but cf. Kümmel, *Introd.*, p. 114.

against the Gnostics. Taken in association with the points noted by earlier scholars, such as the materialisation of Jesus' form in the resurrection narrative or the emphasis upon his eating and drinking with his disciples after the Resurrection, this amounts to a strong case. The one question is whether this is the whole of Luke's purpose in writing. Jeremias for example regards the anti-Docetic use of the post-Resurrection meal as secondary to its significance as a mark of forgiveness, of the disciples' restoration to fellowship with their Master.[23] It is indeed probably a mistake to narrow down Luke's aim in writing to a single purpose, as if he had but one object in mind and no other; it is more likely that he had several aims in view, and even that some of the factors which influenced his writing were not consciously present to his mind. The important points for our purpose are the resemblances to the situation reflected in the Pastorals, and the difference from the approach of the Fourth Evangelist to much the same problem.[24]

The Fourth Gospel raises questions which have been warmly debated. On the one hand, some scholars are naturally reluctant to admit any suggestion that a Gospel so beloved might be tainted with even the least suspicion of the Gnostic heresy. On the other hand there are many, from different schools of thought, who are prepared to recognise at least some affinity between John and the Gnostics. F. C. Grant, for example, suggests that the author 'may have been a Gnostic—a "converted" Gnostic, perhaps.'[25] C. H. Dodd wrote[26] 'there is a sense in which orthodox Christian theologians like Clement of Alexandria and Origen, on the one hand, and Hellenistic Jews like Philo, and pagan writers like the Hermetists, on the other, should be called Gnostics . . . *In this sense* the Gospel according to John should be classed as Gnostic,' (italics mine). And this of course takes no account as yet of Bultmann and his school. More recently, C. K. Barrett has said 'That there exists a relation of some kind between the Fourth Gospel and non-Christian Gnosticism is scarcely open to question; exactly what this relation is,

[23] *The Eucharistic Words of Jesus*, (ET: London 1966), p. 204 n. 3.
[24] Cf. Talbert, pp. 46 f.; C. K. Barrett, *Luke the Historian in Recent Study*, (London 1961), pp. 62 f.
[25] *The Gospels. Their Origin and their Growth*, (London 1959), p. 160.
[26] *The Interpretation of the Fourth Gospel*, p. 97.

is one of the most disputed problems in current New Testament scholarship.'[27]

Here it is well to get back to established facts. (1) The earliest known commentary on the Fourth Gospel was written by the Gnostic Heracleon, and it is the Gnostics who provide us with the first clear traces of a knowledge of John. On the other hand, as Barrett pertinently remarks, it cannot be claimed that their use of the Gospel notably affected their systems, since their interest was largely cosmological and concentrated on the Prologue. 'It is difficult to resist the view that the Gnostics used John because out of it, by exegesis sound or unsound, they were able to win support and enrichment for preconceived theories and mythologies.'[28] Gnostic use of a document does not make the document itself Gnostic.

(2) As already noted, the First Epistle of John provides some of the clearest traces in the New Testament of an incipient Gnosticism. Whether or not the Epistle and the Gospel come from the same author, they certainly derive from the same school. Hence it is probable that the evangelist was aware of the kind of thinking and way of life which are attacked in the Epistle. Recent investigations however have focused attention upon three points which require to be taken into account in this connection: (a) the parallels and resemblances between John and the Dead Sea Scrolls have shown that much which formerly was thought to be Hellenistic was in fact current also in Palestine, at least in certain circles. It would of course be going too far to relate John simply and solely to Palestine and the Qumran sect, but it is no longer possible to treat the Gospel as a purely Hellenistic document. (b) It has been observed that Bultmann's commentary, which attempts to interpret the Gospel against the background of Gnostic dualism, shows 'that at every crucial point the Gospel is in tension with the Gnostic point of view, indeed repudiates it',[29] and indeed this is confirmed by the relevant sections of Bultmann's *Theology*. The Gospel therefore ought *not* to be described as Gnostic without qualification. (c)

[27] *Current Issues in NT Interpretation*, ed. Klassen and Snyder, (London 1962), p. 210.

[28] C. K. Barrett, *The Gospel according to St. John*, (London 1958), p. 55.

[29] Stephen Neill, *The Interpretation of the New Testament 1861–1961*, (London 1964), p. 310.

In a comparison of the theological vocabulary of John with that of the Gospel of Truth, C. K. Barrett[30] brings out the differences between the two works. The eschatological motif, for example, is missing from the Gnostic Gospel, which also diagnoses the human situation in terms of ignorance rather than of sin.[31] The differences indeed 'show the fundamentally biblical and anti-Gnostic content of John.' Similarly Haenchen, after noting the affinities between John and Gnosis, also points out certain differences: if the presentation of Jesus as one who comes from God and returns to God, and whose work consists in his proclamation of the unknown Father, recalls the Gnostic 'emissary'; if it is only those who come to know God in Jesus who are saved; yet on the other side John knows nothing of a fall of divine sparks into matter, and above all there are two major points of variance: the linking of salvation not to a mythical incarnation of the Gnostic cry of awakening but to the word of the historical Jesus, and the fact that Jesus proclaims not the identity of a divine spark in man with God, so that knowledge of God and knowledge of the self become identical, but the gracious God himself.

John then is not Gnostic, although there are certain affinities and the precise relationship is difficult to define. In particular, there is the problem of the evangelist's 'Gnostic' terminology. On this two things require to be said: (1) regard must be paid to the distinction drawn above between the descriptive use of this term and the use which implies derivation. Is this terminology described as Gnostic because it *later* becomes current in the Gnostic systems, or was it already Gnostic, and in what sense, before it was used by John? (2) As already noted, Dodd and others have recognised that there is a sense, a broad and comprehensive sense, in which John *can* be called 'Gnostic'. Indeed, this is one of the points at which the distinction made earlier between Gnosis and Gnosticism is of value. But this broader sense itself requires investigation and more careful definition. Some elements in the Hellenistic Gnosis can be, and should be, more precisely identified as Stoic or Platonic,

[30] *Current Issues*, [see n. 27] pp. 210 ff.
[31] ibid., p. 214. On Bultmann's elimination of the futuristic element from the Johannine eschatology cf. P. Ricca, *Die Eschatologie des vierten Evangeliums*, (Zürich 1966), p. 50 n. 124.

Babylonian, Iranian or Jewish constituents in the contemporary syncretism. Allowance must be made for the convergence of ideas, for the natural tendency to assimilate or even identify similar features in distinct cultural traditions, as was done by those who claimed that the Greeks borrowed from Moses. In short, we must ask whether John's Gnostic terminology is Gnostic only in the descriptive sense, in which case the later Gnostics may have borrowed from John; or implies derivation, either in the sense that John is combatting the incipient Gnosticism of his opponents with their own weapons or, more generally, and more vaguely, that he is using the language of his period, a language marked by the tendencies broadly characterised as Gnosis. And further, we must consider whether John's use of such terminology is in fact Gnostic, or whether this terminology only becomes Gnostic in a strictly Gnostic context.

The burning problem in discussion of Gnosticism and the New Testament always comes with John—and with Paul. The latter indeed presents the more intricate problem, since we have evidence from other sources to indicate that by the end of the first century, the probable date of the Fourth Gospel, an incipient Gnosticism was already developing. As Barrett notes, 'it is for many reasons unlikely that a non-Christian Gnosticism arose full-grown between the writing of John and the writing of the Gospel of Truth in such a way as to influence the author of the latter.'[32] Even if we admit the view that the Gospel of Truth pre-supposes the developed Valentinian theory (see Chapter IV), and must therefore be dated somewhat later, we still have the space of barely half a century between John and Valentinus, and into this we should have to compress the whole development of Ophitism and of the teachings of such men as Saturninus and Basilides, some of which manifestly influenced the development of Valentinianism. It therefore seems a legitimate inference that the origins of Gnosticism proper are pre-Johannine, although here we are moving into the shadowy no-man's-land between Gnosticism proper and the vaguer Gnosis. The problem is to determine how much further back we must go.

If Haenchen's argument could be sustained,[33] that Simon

---

[32] ibid., p. 223.

[33] *Gott und Mensch*, (Tübingen 1965), pp. 265 ff. [=*ZTK* 49, (1952), pp. 316 ff.]. But cf. Wilson, *The Gnostic Problem*, (London 1958), p. 99.

Magus was already a Gnostic before he came into contact with Christianity, then the problem would be resolved; for in Acts the episode of Simon precedes the conversion of Paul. This however involves (a) assumptions regarding the reliability of Acts which not every scholar would be prepared to entertain; and (b) the ever-present problem of definition, for while Simon may reasonably be described as a Gnostic in the sense of Gnosis it is by no means clear that he was a Gnostic in the sense of the later developed Gnosticism. We cannot for example assume that the Megale Apophasis, cited by Hippolytus but apparently unknown to Irenaeus, is a genuinely Simonian document in the sense that it derives from Simon himself; we have to allow for developments within the Simonian school, so that this document may reflect the influences of a much later period.

We are thus reduced to the examination of Paul's own writings in the effort to determine to what extent he reflects or is influenced by Gnosis, as more broadly defined, or even perhaps provides indications of the existence in his life-time of the germ of what later blossomed into Gnosticism. Since Ephesians and Colossians present a special problem, quite apart from questions of authenticity, consideration of these will be deferred for the moment.

At this point attention should be drawn to the careful wording of Haenchen's article: Paul's teaching about the fall of Creation (Rom. 8.19–22) and of Adam (Rom. 5.12–17), about the contrast of ψυχικοί and πνευματικοί (1 Cor. 2.14 f.; 15.21, 44–49), about φῶς and σκότος (Rom. 13.11–13; 1 Thess. 5.4–6) and the demonic rulers of this age (1 Cor. 2.6–8; 2 Cor. 4.4) and the dangers of marriage (1 Cor. 7.32–4, 38) shows 'traits akin to Gnosis'. Again, his doctrine of the Redeemer 'is in contact with the Gnostic doctrine', in that Jesus is presented as a heavenly being who descends unknown (1 Cor. 2.8) from God and returns again to Him (2. Cor. 8.9; Phil. 2.6–11). Other features 'recall' Gnostic theories. The spirit-ruled Christians of 1 Cor. 3.16 and Rom. 8.9 'look like' the Gnostic πνευματικοί.

What does this mean? What do these 'traits akin to Gnosis' signify—that they are derived from Gnosis, or merely like it, or starting-points for it? What is meant by 'contact with Gnostic doctrine'—a fully-developed Gnostic Redeemer-myth? These features certainly 'recall' Gnostic ideas, but was Gnosticism or

even Gnosis the source from which they came? Or have we to do
with Gnostic influence, or merely with Gnostic parallels? Or is
it even possible that at some points reflection on Paul's own
teaching may have led later Gnostics to embellish their own
theories with choice stones quarried from his letters? It should
be noted that, whatever careless readers may have made of his
words, Haenchen does not affirm that these traits *are* Gnostic.
Clearly we have here a task as yet unfinished, calling for careful
exploration and evaluation on sound principles of exegesis. A
wholesale and sweeping incorporation of Paul, and the New
Testament writers generally, into the sphere of 'Gnosticism' is
not adequate; nor is an equally wholesale and sweeping rejection of any kind of contact whatsoever. Our task calls for long
and patient evaluation and assessment. Some features, like the
contrast of light and darkness, may be more or less common-
place in Hellenistic thought; others, like that of the demonic
rulers of this age, may have links with Jewish apocalyptic;
others again may perhaps be documented from Greek philosophy. All these may legitimately be classed for convenience of
reference under the general head of Gnosis; but this is not yet
Gnosticism.

Paul in short stands at a point of inter-play and inter-action,
where ideas from various distinct cultural traditions were in
circulation. In some cases the conceptions in two different
traditions might in fact be identical, and therefore readily
assimilated. In other cases however the conceptions though
similar were not identical, and their assimilation produced a
modification, sometimes profound, on one side or the other; or
the associations which clustered around a conception in one
tradition introduced a new element into the understanding of
the corresponding conception in a different tradition. The
Septuagint, to come to a concrete example, presents the Hebrew
Scriptures in a Greek dress but, says Dodd, 'the words of the
Hebrew Scriptures, in passing into Greek, partly lost one set of
associations, and partly gained a new set, while at the same
time the Greek words used in translation may have acquired
something of the value of the Hebrew words they represent.'[34]
This, as Dodd shows, is of some significance for the understanding of the Old Testament, and of the Jewish religion, by

[34] *The Bible and the Greeks*, (London 1935), p. xi.

Diaspora Jews who read their Scriptures in Greek, or for that matter by Gentiles who may have had no other means of access to the Jewish faith. The process however did not affect the Jews alone, or their religion. It has long been noted that the only mystery religions from the East which enjoyed any large measure of success in the Graeco-Roman world were those which were capable of some degree of Hellenisation. We have only to envisage two men of different cultural backgrounds and different language, whose only common medium of communication was Greek, comparing and discussing their respective religions, to realise the extent of the possibilities for assimilation and syncretism. And on its entry upon the stage of the wider world Christianity had to be 'translated' from its original Palestinian thought-forms and terms of reference into those comprehensible in its new environment. It is not in the least surprising that there should have been some people who in the process lost the essence of the Gospel in 'the maelstrom of Hellenistic syncretism.' For convenience in study and analysis, we have to talk in terms of ideas, trends and currents of thought; but in fact we are dealing with ideas in the minds of *people*, which introduces a highly complicating factor into all our investigations.

A further point to be noted arises in connection with Haenchen's discussion of the Corinthian correspondence. Paul, he says, combats the Gnostics in Corinth because they denied a future resurrection of the body in favour of a present resurrection in the Spirit. Citing as evidence 1 Cor. 15.29–32 and 2. Cor. 5.1–5, he adds that Paul 'at first misunderstood the Gnostic teaching because of inadequate information.' This in the present context, assuming for the moment that Paul *was* dealing with Gnostics, is a legitimate inference. There is a difference in the positions held in the two letters, although C. F. D. Moule[35] has recently argued a different exegesis, that there was a change in Paul's own ideas on the subject: in 1 Corinthians he is thinking of the spiritual body as a kind of overcoat, to be put on *on top of* the existing material body, whereas in 2 Corinthians he is contemplating the more painful, drastic and demanding prospect that the material must be annihilated before the spiritual body can be put on. In the latter case Paul would be approaching

[35] *NTS* 12, (1966), pp. 106 ff.

the Gnostic conception which seems to underlie a passage in the Gospel of Philip, although it should be added that this passage starts from Paul's own teaching.

The point for our present purpose is however that while Haenchen's inference may be legitimate here it is not universally valid. To hold a mirror up to Paul, in the hope of detecting Gnostic leanings in his opponents, is one thing. To decide, when the evidence is not forthcoming, that Paul misunderstood his opponents and was entertaining Gnostics unawares, is quite another; for this may involve the reading into the theories deduced from Paul's refutations of the very Gnostic teachings for which we are looking. 'Gnostic influences' which have first to be read into the evidence are a very insecure foundation on which to build.

In the above discussion it has been assumed for the moment that Paul was dealing with Gnostics, but this is precisely the point at issue. Here the perennial problem of definition rises once again. In the broad and comprehensive sense of the term Gnosis, it is perfectly correct to speak of Gnosis at Corinth; but this is not really very helpful unless we can determine the relation between this Gnosis and the later developed Gnosticism. To speak of Gnosis in Corinth, and then to interpret the teaching of Paul's opponents by a wholesale introduction of ideas from the second-century systems, is to run the risk of seriously distorting the whole picture. There *are* points of contact, and indeed the very least that can be said is probably Robert Law's remark[36] that 1 Corinthians shows 'into how congenial a soil the seeds of Gnosticism were about to fall.' Yet prior to the sowing, and even when the sowing has been completed, the most fertile field may be some way short of being ripe for the harvest. It is therefore necessary to ask whether those features of the Corinthian 'heresy' which are claimed as Gnostic are in fact already Gnostic in the stricter sense of the term, whether they are the germs out of which the later Gnosticism developed, or whether they admit of some other explanation. These alternatives, of course, are not all mutually exclusive.

To take but two examples: (a) it is frequently affirmed that on the question of the resurrection Paul's opponents, like the

[36] *The Tests of Life*, (Edinburgh 1909), p. 28.

heretics of the Pastorals, maintained that it had already taken place.[37] This may be so; but on the other hand this interpretation may be no more than a reading back from the Pastorals into the situation at Corinth. The most natural rendering of 1 Cor. 15.12 is not that some say there will be no resurrection (because it is already past), but that in their view there is no such thing. The verb is in the present tense, not the future. In other words, Paul's opponents would be maintaining the 'Greek' view of the immortality of the soul over against a resurrection of the body, as indeed Paul's whole argument seems to imply, with its emphasis on the fact of the resurrection of Jesus. Robertson and Plummer[38] appositely quote a passage from Aeschylus (Eum. 648): οὔτις ἔστ᾽ ἀνάστασις. Moreover it is possible to see how the heresy of the Pastorals could have developed from a misunderstanding of Paul's own teaching: in Rom. 6 he speaks of the Christian being buried with Christ in Baptism, of the old man being crucified, of walking in newness of life. In this context Paul speaks of our being σύμφυτοι καὶ τῆς ἀναστάσεως in the future (Rom. 6.5), but it is not difficult to see how the conclusion could have been drawn that the resurrection had already taken place.

(b) It has been argued that the 'wisdom' section in 1 Cor. 1–2 reflects a pre-Christian Gnostic Sophia myth.[39] Now the figure of Sophia does play a prominent part in the later Gnostic systems, and there are grounds for carrying the beginnings of such speculation back at least to the Jewish Wisdom literature of the inter-testamental period. This does not however necessarily mean that Paul had any such myth consciously in mind as he wrote, or even that he was unconsciously influenced by it. This is a point where Jonas' warning against the conveyor-belt analogy is highly apposite: we cannot assume that if a theory is older than Paul it was therefore known to him, and must have been alluded to whenever he touched on the subject. Modern

[37] Cf. e.g. Kümmel, *An die Korinther*, (*Hbuch z. NT*, Tübingen 1949), pp. 192 f., and contrast Lietzmann's own view in the original commentary [ibid., p. 79].

[38] *1 Corinthians*, (*ICC*, Edinburgh 1953), p. 347.

[39] Cf. U. Wilckens, *Weisheit und Torheit*, (Tübingen 1959), with Köster's review in *Gnomon* 33, (1961), pp. 590 ff.; also Wilckens' art. σοφία in Kittel *TWB*, vii, pp. 465 ff., 497 ff. For critical assessment see K. Prümm in *ZKT* 87, (1965), pp. 399 ff.; 88, (1966), pp. 1 ff.

scholars, with a much greater concern for fullness of documentation and adequate coverage of the relevant material, have
been known to overlook discussions which they had actually
read, or pieces of evidence of which they knew. In Paul's case,
such an occurrence is the more likely in that he was writing less
formally and not trying to explore every avenue. Moreover his
whole discussion begins from an Old Testament quotation
which seems to have no connection with any Sophia myth, and
it can be quite adequately expounded, without introducing a
hypostatised Wisdom at all, in terms of the wisdom upon which
men pride themselves and the 'foolishness' of God which yet is
superior to all the wisdom of this world. It is only the identification of Christ as 'the power of God and the wisdom of God'
which prompts the question of 'Gnostic' influence, in the sense
that Paul is claiming for Christ the titles and attributes applied
by his opponents to their hypostatised Sophia; but the alternative surely bears examination, that the identification arises
naturally out of the context of the whole discussion.

Space does not permit of detailed discussion of the whole
Corinthian question, but these examples may suffice to show
that while there may at Corinth have been certain affinities
with the later Gnosticism a thorough-going 'Gnostic' interpretation of the situation may involve some begging of the question.
A further problem arises with 2 Corinthians: is Paul dealing
with the same opponents? Or is he dealing in one case with
opponents of a Gnostic type, in the other with Jewish Christians,
or with Judaisers?[40] Can we assume that Paul throughout his
career was confronted with the same kind of opposition, or did
he at different periods and in different areas have to face attack
from different quarters? The Tübingen school saw the whole
history of the early Church in terms of a conflict between the
Judaising and the Hellenistic wings. More recently the attempt
has been made, particularly by W. Schmithals,[41] to identify
Paul's opponents in almost every case as Gnostics. In the broad
sense of the term, perhaps they were; even in Galatia, where all
the evidence suggests rather a Judaising opposition, there are

[40] See D. Georgi, *Die Gegner des Paulus im 2 Korintherbrief*, (Neukirchen
1964).

[41] *Die Gnosis in Korinth*, (Göttingen 1956); *Paulus und die Gnostiker*,
(Hamburg-Bergstedt 1965).

certain elements of a 'Gnostic' type.[42] But to describe all Paul's opponents as Gnostic without further qualification is to ignore distinctions which both can and ought to be made, and to run the risk of interpreting the embryonic and undeveloped in the light of the mature and fully developed systems of a later age. It seems much nearer to the facts to recognise Judaisers in Galatia, with perhaps some 'Gnostic' leanings, opponents of a more Gnostic type at Corinth, with perhaps a Jewish Christian element which may have entered into the situation at a later stage.

Ephesians and Colossians present special problems, in the matter of date and authenticity as well as in regard to possible 'Gnostic' influences. Some scholars regard both as Pauline, others consider them both deutero-Pauline, others again accept the one but not the other, Colossians as a rule being given the stronger claim. Obviously, our decision on such questions must affect our interpretation of developments in Paul's own life-time and in the succeeding generation; but here again we must beware of arguing in a circle. Again, if Günther Bornkamm can write[43] 'Of the fact that behind the Colossian heresy there stands a Jewish or Judaistic Gnosis, strongly infected by Iranian ideas, there can scarcely be any doubt', Ernst Percy argues[44] that this heresy *lacks* the characteristic and essential features of Gnosticism, and A. S. Peake long ago[45] roundly denied any Gnostic influence, declaring it improbable that we have Gnosticism here even in a rudimentary form. 'We are certain,' he

---

[42] Cf. Paul's references to 'the weak and beggarly elements' [Gal. 4.3 ff.; but see also *The Gnostic Problem*, p. 93 n. 111], and his warnings against transforming liberty into licence. The facts which led Lütgert, Ropes, Schmithals and others to see Gnosticism in some form in Galatia require explanation, but do they indicate a developed *system* or merely the raw material out of which such systems were to be built? See further A. Oepke, *Der Brief an die Galater*, (Berlin 1957), pp. 93 ff. The reference to 'this present evil age' [Gal. 1.4] should be linked with Jewish apocalyptic rather than with Gnosticism [cf. Oepke p. 19; Burton, *Galatians*, (ICC, Edinburgh 1921), pp. 426 ff.; Sasse in *TWB*, i, p. 206].

[43] *Das Ende des Gesetzes*, (Munich 1958), p. 150.

[44] *Probleme der Kolosser- und Epheserbriefe*, (Lund 1946), pp. 176 ff.

[45] *Expositor's Greek Testament*, iii, (London 1903), pp. 484 ff. See further H. Hegermann, *Die Vorstellung vom Schöpfungsmittler im hellenistischen Judentum und Urchristentum*, (TU 82, Berlin 1961); H. M. Schenke in ZTK 61, (1964), pp. 391 ff.

says, 'of the Jewish nature of the teaching, and if it can be explained from Judaism alone have no warrant for calling in other sources.' A further complication is introduced by the contacts noted between the Colossian heresy and Qumran.[46] Close on a century ago J. B. Lightfoot[47] linked the Colossian heresy with the Essenes, a view which Peake was to reject. Were the Essenes Gnostic after all? Or have we at Qumran and at Colossae still only 'Gnosticism in the making', or even nothing more than the first tentative experiments in combining the raw materials? It should be noted also that passages from both Ephesians and Colossians were later re-interpreted by the second-century Gnostics to suit their own purposes. One passage in Irenaeus' account of Valentinianism (adv. Haer. 1.1.4) looks very like an adaptation of Col. 1.19,[48] and others will be noted in the next chapter.

According to Haenchen,[49] Colossians 'probably pre-supposes a Jewish-Christian Gnosis, which did indeed ascribe to Christ the work of redemption but demanded the worship of the elemental powers ($\sigma\tauοιχεῖα τοῦ κόσμου$ 2.8,20) who with him form the Pleroma (cf. 1.19; 2.9 f.).' In none of the verses cited, however, is it expressly said that these powers form part of the Pleroma—this is an inference in the light of later Gnostic thought. Indeed, the Valentinian technical use of this term for the totality of the higher aeons is sometimes extended, for convenience, to describe the spiritual world in systems which do not themselves make use of the word. It is at least open to question whether the 'Gnostic' interpretation of such passages in Colossians would ever have been suggested but for our prior knowledge of the use of the term in Valentinianism; and consideration of the range of possible meanings would suggest that this is not the only possible interpretation.[50] On the other hand the word does seem to be used in a technical sense at some points in Ephesians and Colossians, and there seems to be

[46] Cf. W. D. Davies, *Christian Origins and Judaism*, (London 1962), p. 157. For Ephesians cf. K. G. Kuhn, *NTS* 7, (1961), pp. 334 ff.

[47] *St. Paul's Epistles to the Colossians and Philemon*, (London 1875), esp. pp. 83 ff.

[48] Cf. Sagnard, *La gnose valentinienne*, (Paris 1947), p. 605.

[49] RGG³ II, col. 1654.

[50] Cf. Bauer, *Wörterbuch* and *TWB* s.v.; also C. F. D. Moule, *Colossians and Philemon*, (Cambridge 1957), pp. 164 ff.

justification for the view suggested by Ernest Best,[51] that the Hellenistic philosophical conception of the universe as filled by God was at this time passing into the Gnostic conception of a divine *pleroma*, at once the abode of the aeons and the aggregate of them. In this case we should have in this conception one of the 'points of growth' for the later Gnosticism.

Again, Haenchen speaks of the use in Colossians, in a Christianised form, of 'the Gnostic idea of the Redeemer as the Urmensch, identical with the cosmos.' In Ephesians 4.8–10 he finds 'the Gnostic doctrine of the descent and ascent of the Redeemer', who at 2.15 appears as the 'new Man' and at 4.13 as ἀνὴρ τέλειος, which Haenchen identifies as the Urmensch. Further traces of the Gnostic Anthropos doctrine are found in the statements about Christ as the head of the body (Eph. 4.3 f., 12; 5.23), while the description of the Church as a heavenly building (2.20–22) and its relation to Wisdom (3.8–10) are 'akin to Gnostic ideas'. Once again it is advisable to call a halt and ask what precisely is meant. Does kinship with Gnostic ideas imply derivation from Gnosticism, or merely that the same kind of imagery is employed on one side and on the other? Ideas of a Heavenly Man or Primal Man are admittedly pre-Christian, but a considerable leap of faith is involved in the assumption that these pre-Christian ideas already carried with them the full implications of the alleged Gnostic Redeemer-myth. Summing up recent studies, P. Pokorny[52] writes that an original pre-Gnostic Urmensch-Redeemer myth cannot be proved, and that the use of Gnostic texts for the exegesis of Ephesians and Colossians, especially in regard to the conception of the Body, has become problematical. Building on the researches of Schenke and others, he develops a theory of an Anthropos-myth, based on Jewish speculation about Gen. 1.26 f., which is quite another matter than the old Redeemer-myth hypothesis. Here again we may have one of the points of growth for later Gnostic thinking. As Best puts it,[53] 'once Paul had attached the metaphor of the body and its members to Christ, it was only to be expected that Gnosticism would attach it to the Heavenly Man and so produce the references we have to it.' The Pauline use of the

---

[51] *One Body in Christ*, (London 1955), p. 148, cf. p. 140.
[52] Petr Pokorný, *Die Epheserbrief und die Gnosis*, (Berlin 1965), p. 40.
[53] op. cit., p. 87 n. 1 [see generally pp. 85 ff.].

E

metaphor in his earlier epistles may have provided a part of the
stimulus which led to later developments, although this is not to
say that it was by any means the only factor.

This survey is by no means exhaustive, but may serve for
present purposes. It is evident that if we approach from the side
of the second Christian century, and interpret in the light of the
later Gnostic systems, there is much in the New Testament that
may be claimed as 'Gnostic'. When we begin at the other end,
however, and endeavour to trace the historical development, it
is another matter. In most cases the 'Gnostic' features admit of
another interpretation, and seldom if ever is the Gnostic explanation absolutely demanded as the one explanation which
alone is possible. If we think in terms of the wider definition of
Gnosis, again, the New Testament belongs in the 'Gnostic' sphere;
but this is to obscure distinctions which ought to be made.
On the one hand, 'Gnosis' may be a convenient label for the
general trend, but frequently it is possible to identify more
precisely the source from which a particular idea is derived.
'Gnosis' thus tends to become little more than an attitude,
finding expression in ideas drawn from various sources, and it is
frequently difficult in the extreme to determine to what extent
this attitude is actually present at all. On the other hand, the
New Testament reveals a variety of response and re-action to
what appears to be a developing movement. Unless we begin by
pre-supposing Gnostics at every turn, there is nothing Paul's
letters to Thessalonica or Philippi which demands a 'Gnostic'
explanation. Nor is there in James or 1 Peter. Galatians shows
some vague traces of the kind of thinking later characteristic of
Gnosticism, but it is by no means beyond question that the
warning against license in the closing chapters was directed
against anti-cosmic libertarian Gnostics; it is obviously quite
possible that some could have misinterpreted freedom from the
law to mean complete absence of moral restraint, without
actually being Gnostics. Corinth supplies a better case, and at
least reveals how easily Gnostic ideas could develop. Somewhat
clearer signs appear in Ephesians and Colossians, but even here
much is still vague and ambiguous. It is still in debate whether
the false teaching in view is Gnostic or Jewish, or both. And this
seems to hold in general for Paul's life-time and the immediately
succeeding period.

Greater clarity and assurance comes only when we approach the end of the century. In 1 John and the Pastorals we find for the first time real traces of what may be called Gnosticism proper, although even here, and in the Pastorals particularly, the evidence is not always so firm as one might wish. The implication seems to be that Gnosticism in the proper sense developed alongside Christianity in the course of the first century, and that this was a time of considerable ferment, during which nothing was in any sense final or clear-cut. The fact that so often it is difficult to decide whether some feature is Gnostic or Jewish, and the marked Jewish element in later Gnostic thinking, may suggest that there was a Jewish Gnosticism before there was a Christian, and hence that the origins of Gnosticism proper go back to the pre-Christian period; but here we are moving beyond what can be established on the basis of the New Testament evidence into the realm of conjecture. In terms of the distinction drawn at the Messina Colloquium, it may be said that there is ample justification for the pre-Gnostic position, that there were in existence in pre-Christian times various themes and motifs, conceptions and ideas, which later were incorporated into Gnosticism proper, but that at this stage they cannot be said to constitute 'Gnosticism' in the strict sense.

In this connection it has finally to be noted that the identification of 'Gnostic terminology' is a dubious expedient.[54] The examples cited, and in particular such words as $\pi\lambda\acute{\eta}\rho\omega\mu\alpha$ and $\tau\acute{\epsilon}\lambda\epsilon\iota\sigma$, show that while they did acquire a technical sense in later Gnosticism this sense is not the only one possible, and sometimes is not even probable, when the word occurs in the New Testament. To import into a New Testament passage the interpretation given to it by the Gnostics may be to distort the meaning, and the same holds for the terminology. Of the seventeen New Testament occurrences of $\pi\lambda\acute{\eta}\rho\omega\mu\alpha$, as examination of the concordance will reveal, only a few are capable of interpretation in Gnostic terms, and none absolutely require it to the exclusion of all other meanings. We have to distinguish those areas in which 'Gnostic influence' is clear and unmistakable from those in which it is merely possible, and from those again in which the possibility is distinctly remote.

[54] Cf. S. Laeuchli, *The Language of Faith*, (Nashville 1962; London 1965).

III

Gnostic Use of the New Testament

THE preceding chapter has clearly shown that the relation between the New Testament on the one hand and the Gnostic movement on the other is by no means a simple one. If we approach the New Testament from the side of the second century, there is much that is familiar, much that lends itself to interpretation in the light of the developed Gnostic theories; and it is then very natural to assume, as the explanation for these phenomena, a pre-Christian Gnosticism which has exercised an extensive influence upon the New Testament writers. On the other hand, (1) there is no conclusive proof of the existence of a fully-developed Gnosticism in the pre-Christian period; (2) some of the material quoted as evidence for Gnostic influence does not in itself demand an exclusively Gnostic interpretation, but can equally be understood in quite non-Gnostic terms; and (3) some of this material can be traced back to other movements of thought, to the Old Testament or to the Jewish apocalyptic or wisdom literature, to some school of Greek philosophy, be it Platonism, Stoicism, or Pythagoreanism, or to one or another of the religious traditions of the ancient East. It is therefore essential to consider at every point whether the Gnostic connotation is necessary to any given term or concept, inherent in it from the beginning, or is the result of a later re-interpretation imposed upon it within a Gnostic context. It may indeed be convenient to use some such term as Gnosis as a general label for the whole phenomenon, but use of the adjective Gnostic without qualification is frankly dangerous.

In this connection it may be objected that to distinguish between Gnosticism proper and Gnosis in this wider and vaguer sense is to introduce unnecessary complications, and that to insist on identifying particular elements specifically as Stoic, Platonic or Jewish rather than Gnostic is merely to complicate matters further. On this it must be said in the first place that while there is a continuity between the vaguer Gnosis and the developed Gnosticism, the two are not identical in such a way that what is true of the second may also be predicated, without qualification, of the first. There are elements in the developed second-century systems for which we have as yet no evidence in the early wider Gnosis, in particular the marked anti-cosmic strain, the conception of the Demiurge as a subordinate deity hostile to man, the hostility to the Jewish God. To understand the growth of Gnosticism proper, and of the later Gnosis, we have to investigate the reasons for the developments which have taken place.

Secondly, while the Stoic, Platonic, Jewish or other elements do indeed become Gnostic at a later stage, indiscriminate use of this label tends to deprive it of any real significance. Everything in the thought of the early Christian centuries becomes Gnostic, regardless of the fact that some of the writers concerned were outspokenly opponents of Gnosticism. Philo, Paul, John, Clement of Alexandria, Origen and Plotinus are grouped together under the same head as Valentinus, Basilides, Marcion and the writers of the Nag Hammadi documents. Yet to ignore the differences is quite as serious an error as neglect of similarities. It may appear to be simpler to use a single label, glossing over the finer academic distinctions, but when appeal is made to the principle of Occam's razor that principle is not always cited in full: *entia non sunt multiplicanda praeter necessitatem.* It is not the multiplication of hypothetical sources which is to be avoided, but their *unnecessary* multiplication; and in the present instance it is open to question whether application of the principle is even valid; for Platonism, Stoicism and the rest are not hypothetical sources, but are already present and can be shown to be the sources of particular ideas. The only hypothetical entity, in fact, is the pre-Christian Gnosticism which is so often held to have been so widely influential. Gnosis may serve as a convenient and legitimate label for a whole complex of related phenomena; but Gnosis is not yet Gnosticism. If there is continuity and development, there has also been modification and re-interpretation.

A further point to emerge is that in the New Testament period we have to take account not only of influence from this vaguer Gnosis but also of reaction against it, and against the incipient forms of the later Gnosticism. How far we can really speak of Gnosticism in the first half-century after the Crucifixion is very much open to question, although the 'points of growth' are certainly present. Much depends here on our interpretation of the situation at Corinth, and on the date and authenticity of Ephesians and Colossians. Were the latter genuine letters of Paul, and the false teachers opposed in them recognisably Gnostic, we should have stronger grounds for dating the origins of Gnosticism proper into Paul's own life-time. As it is, the earliest clear indications of the emergence of an incipient Gnosticism appear to fall in the last quarter of the first century. This fits well with Grant's theory of the disappointed hopes of Qumran sectarians after the Fall of Jerusalem in A.D. 70, although as already noted this is probably not the whole answer. There were other developments still to take place.

The first century, then, presents a rather confused picture, with an emergent Christianity seeking to establish itself on the stage of a wider world, endeavouring to understand and express its faith in language comprehensible to the people of that world, defending itself first against enemies from without and later also against the subversive activities of enemies within. Which was eventually to become the orthodox tradition, and which the heretical, was still an open question. Equally open for us is the further question, whether there was anything so distinct that it can be called a movement, in competition with Christianity and with the other religions of the time, which later developed into the classical Gnosticism; or whether the precursor of Gnosticism at this stage was no more than a number of varied trends and tendencies. To use the distinction drawn at the Messina Colloquim, the proto-Gnostic view would affirm the first, while the pre-Gnostic would regard either position as tenable. In the second century however the lines of cleavage become gradually more distinct, the Gnostic religion is more and more clearly recognised as a rival to the Christian faith, the more dangerous in that it has so much in common and yet is so fundamentally different. At this stage part of the common element is provided by the New Testament itself, for it was used by 'orthodox' and Gnostic alike, although sometimes with very different results.

The history of exegesis is as yet to a large extent a field uncultivated, in certain areas indeed almost virgin soil. We have of course studies of particular themes and concepts, or of particular texts, as they are handled by various expositors down the centuries. We have also discussions of the allegorical method, generally in the context of an examination of the exegesis of a Philo of Alexandria or an Origen, and we have studies of the exegetical methods of particular Fathers in the context of surveys of their life and work. But much of this material is dispersed in numerous volumes, if not buried in periodicals and *Festschriften*, where it is difficult even for the specialist to trace it. It would be difficult to name one volume which provides at once a comprehensive survey of the whole history of biblical exegesis and sufficient detailed discussion of specific points.[1] Yet this is surely a field of genuine importance for those whose task it is to expound the Scriptures. How was it done by the men of the past? What can we learn from them, from their errors as well as from their achievements? What are the canons of sound exegesis, how and when were they arrived at, to what extent have they been observed or neglected in days gone by? It is encouraging to learn that a new series of publications recently launched in Germany is devoted to this very purpose.[2]

It is not of course the aim of this chapter to supply the need. All that is attempted here is a preliminary and of necessity rather cursory survey of one small corner of a very extensive field. Tertullian in a famous dictum once declared that the heretic Marcion practised Biblical Criticism with a pen-knife, cutting away all that did not conform with his own conception of the Christian faith; but the accusation brought against the Gnostics was a different one, not that they truncated Scripture but that they distorted it to serve their own ends and purposes.[3] This, incidentally, provides further reason for a certain reserve about classifying Marcion unambiguously as a Gnostic.

To bring things into some sort of perspective at the outset, we may begin with two studies published in the present century,

---

[1] A few relevant works are: R. M. Grant, *A Short History of the Interpretation of the Bible*, (New York 1964; London 1965); R. P. C. Hanson, *Allegory and Event*, (London 1959); Beryl Smalley, *The Study of the Bible in the Middle Ages*, (Oxford 1941); W. G. Kümmel, *Das Neue Testament*, (Munich 1958); Stephen Neill, *The Interpretation of the NT 1861–1961*, (London 1964).

[2] *Beiträge zur Geschichte der biblischen Exegese*, (Tübingen: J. C. B. Mohr). There is also a similar series on Hermeneutics.

[3] Cf. H. E. W. Turner, *The Pattern of Christian Truth*, (London 1954), pp. 168 f., 194.

singling out only a few points to serve as guiding lines for our examination of the texts themselves. The first is Carola Barth's study of the interpretation of the New Testament in Valentinian Gnosticism, published in 1911.[4] Here, following upon a survey of the formulae employed in citation, it is noted that for the Valentinians Christ and his apostles speak to reveal the hidden mysteries to the disciples. Their words have an absolute and incontrovertible validity. The formulae of citation already make it clear that it is the Saviour's function as a teacher and revealer of Gnosis which stands in the forefront of his activity. It is also notable that the words of Paul are introduced in the same manner as those of the Lord. Further on it is observed that certain passages show characteristic variations, in which we can detect genuinely Valentinian tendentious modifications. Again, it is noted that events in the life of Jesus, the birth, the baptism, the temptation and so on, are so interpreted as to include more than appears to earthly sight—for parallel with them are *heavenly* events, part of the process of eternal salvation. At later points reference is made to allegorical interpretation, not only of the parables and other words of Jesus but of events from his life, and also of the words of Paul; to the further development of the cosmological statements of the New Testament; and to the use of number-symbolism. There are cases of straightforward simple application of the text, but there are also cases of apologetic interpretation. Towards the end we have this comment: that these exegetes made use of the rules of interpretation current in their time, as we can see by comparing them with Paul, or the interpreters of Homer, or Philo of Alexandria. It is only rarely that we can charge them with arbitrary procedure. The literal interpretation is usually to be found in sections dealing with cosmology or soteriology, or in purely ethical sections. And these Valentinian interpreters have no interest in attaining to a historical grasp of the life of Jesus. This last sentence, incidentally, reflects one of the dominant interests of New Testament scholarship in the period when Barth's book was written.

The picture drawn by Barth is broadly confirmed by the outline of Gnostic exegesis presented by H. E. W. Turner in *The*

---

[4] *Die Interpretation des Neuen Testaments in der valentinianischen Gnosis* (*TU* 37.3, Leipzig 1911).

Pattern of Christian Truth.[5] He notes that there are few references
to incidents of Jesus' life, but much use of parables and hard
sayings. Passages from the Fourth Gospel are of frequent occurrence, but it is used as a source-book rather than a source,
raided for proof-texts without any real attempt to treat it as a
whole—a point confirmed in its turn by the remarks of C. K.
Barrett quoted in the previous chapter.[6] In Paul, selection is
made of the more mysterious passages, and here Turner adds a
noteworthy comment: 'Those who like Bultmann find Gnostic
motifs already present in St. Paul would hold that here they
were merely receiving their own with usury, but it is more
probable that they were selecting isolated "numinous expres-
sions" or perhaps even bridge words with little regard for what
lay on the other side.' To look at it from another angle, there is
no question, as we have already seen, that the terminology and
many of the ideas employed in Gnosticism were already current
in the pre-Christian period, and even certain combinations of
these ideas; but we still have to ask if they already possessed a
Gnostic connotation.

Here the European visitor to America has a useful analogy at
hand, although of course no analogy is ever complete or perfect.
The traveller cannot fail to observe various customs, usages and
other aspects of American life which are already familiar, for
the simple reason that they are part of the heritage from the
settlers of a by-gone age. One cannot however understand 'the
American way of life' merely by tracing back particular elements to their ultimate origins in Europe or elsewhere—due
allowance has to be made for the country itself, its climate, the
heritage of its history. Many factors have contributed to the
moulding of something that is in many ways unique, however
close its affinities with the ways of certain other peoples. Some
elements again have been developed further than in the lands of
their origin, or united with elements from other sources to form
something new; and sometimes the similarities are due not to
European influence upon America but to American influence
upon Europe. So it is with Gnosticism—we must beware of the

[5] *The Pattern of Christian Truth*, pp. 232 ff. Cf. also Norbert Brox, *Offenbarung, Gnosis u. gnostischer Mythos bei Irenäus von Lyon*, (Salzburg 1966), esp.
pp. 56 ff.
[6] See above, p. 46.

facile assumption that the occurrence of a single element, or even a group of elements, is sufficient to demonstrate the existence of anything that may truly be called Gnostic. Where the New Testament is concerned we have to explore not one but many possibilities: direct indebtedness on one side or the other, dependence on some common background of thought and ideas, mutual influence, and so on. In particular we have to allow for the convergence of ideas, for the tendency to assume that what is similar is in fact the same. The Jewish doctrine of the Two Ages, for example, is not identical with the Platonic distinction between the visible world and the intelligible, but the two could be and were confused, and not only in the ancient world.

Further on, Turner notes the Gnostic penchant for numerical symbolism, and 'the flight from history which characterises their systems as a whole'. 'The factual side of the Biblical record is systematically undervalued. Hence arises their persistent neglect of the context in which their quotations are set. Their references to Biblical incident spiritualise away the basis upon which it rests.' Turner later quotes the extract from Theodotus[7] which deals with the teaching method of Jesus: first mystically and typically, secondly by parables and dark sayings, and finally in open revelation. Here it should be noted that the Gnostics were not the only ones to find the parables and sayings obscure: 'for the Primitive Church,' writes Otto Piper,[8] 'the story of Jesus presented no special problem, while they discovered a depth of meaning in his sayings, which was not easily probed.' As words of the Lord, these sayings were significant and important; was it not written 'You have the words of eternal life' (John 6.68)? But detached from the context in which they were originally spoken, sometimes without even a clue to the situation to which they were addressed, they presented a problem to the would-be interpreter. Indeed there are indications of such a situation as early as the canonical Gospels themselves, for example in Mark's section on the significance of the parables (Mk. 4). Transported from Palestine in the time of Jesus into a wider world, and into the situation of a later age, the parables and sayings inevitably became mysterious and enigmatic; but

[7] Clem. Alex., *Excerpta ex Theodoto*, (ed. Casey, London 1934; Sagnard, Paris 1948).
[8] *Princeton Seminary Bulletin* 53, (1959), pp. 19 f.

they were the words of the Lord and words of life, and therefore demanded explanation. 'He who finds the interpretation of these words,' says the Gospel of Thomas (log. 1), 'shall not taste of death.' The same attitude could readily have been adopted by others, not simply towards the sayings recorded in Thomas but towards the teaching of Jesus generally.

At another point Turner compares the methods of Heracleon and Origen.[8a] They are, he says, 'fundamentally at one in their use of symbolic interpretation', but 'the significant feature in the work of Heracleon is not the employment of allegory but the standard of reference which determines its application ... His chief defect lay in importing his own doctrinal pre-suppositions into the text instead of applying himself to the elucidation of the real meaning of his author.' Despite the centuries that have passed, there is something here that is still of relevance. The Warrack lecturer on preaching at the University of St. Andrews in 1964 devoted one of his lectures to '*The Homiletic Sin of Eisegesis*'.[9]

So much for general background. What do the texts reveal— in particular the latest discoveries? At the outset we are faced with a problem of identification. Some of these texts belong quite definitely and unmistakably to *Christian* Gnosticism, and the number of New Testament quotations which they certainly contain makes it the more probable that the doubtful cases should be classed at least as allusions. But what of those texts in which the Christian element is comparatively slight? The Apocalypse of Adam, for example, has a passage about a child born of a virgin who was driven out of his city with his mother and taken to a desert place.[10] Here the editor notes that one might think of Rev. 12.5, or rather of its mythological background. One's instinctive reaction may be to ask 'Why not just Rev. 12.5 alone?'; but this would be to beg the whole question. There are points at which one might be inclined to discover Christian influence in this document, echoes of or allusions to New

---

[8a] Cf. M. Simonetti, *Vetera Christianorum* 3, (1966), pp. 3–75.

[9] James T. Cleland, *Preaching to be Understood*, (Nashville 1965), pp. 59 ff.

[10] Böhlig-Labib, *Koptisch-gnostische Apokalypsen aus Codex V von Nag Hammadi*, (Halle-Wittenburg 1963), p. 111. It should be noted that this is but one of fourteen successive statements about the coming of the Phoster [see Böhlig's discussion, op. cit., pp. 91 ff.].

Testament material, but in no case is such influence incontrovertible; and to limit our attention to possible Christian influence is to commit the very error against which warning was given above in relation to alleged Gnostic influence on the New Testament. The motif of 'the man born to be king', in one form or another, is both old and widespread. In Greek mythology, to go no further afield, there are the stories of Jason and Perseus; and so far as the background of Rev. 12 is concerned there is the legend of the birth of Apollo.[11] From a later age one might also recall, as a parallel to the Apocalypse of Adam, the story in the life of John the Baptist according to Serapion,[12] while in the Old Testament there is the episode of Hagar and Ishmael. But while each of these may show certain points of contact with the passage in the Apocalypse of Adam it would be too much to claim any one of them as its source. Nor should we lay too much stress on the occurrence in this Apocalypse of the word παρθένος, which incidentally does not appear in Rev. 12. If it is to be taken strictly, in the sense of virginity, it would presumably be applicable to Danae, the mother of Perseus; but whether it is to be taken strictly is itself matter for discussion.[13] In short, while we may perhaps suspect an allusion to Rev. 12.5 in the Apocalypse of Adam, we cannot be certain; we have to make allowance for the possibility of other influences.

The Gospel of Thomas presents a different problem, for here our approach will differ according to our decision as to the nature of this document. If we assume it to be based on our Gospels, then it becomes a source of information for Gnostic use of the Gospels; but if we have reason to suspect that any given saying goes back to an independent tradition, then it is another matter. Again, even when we have clear evidence for the use of our New Testament, the allusions may not be easy to detect, or it may be impossible to affirm with confidence that the author had a particular passage in mind when he wrote. When we read in the Gospel of Philip, for example, the words 'Then the slaves

[11] On the interpretation of this passage see P. Prigent, *Apocalypse 12. Histoire de l'exégèse*, (Tübingen 1959).

[12] Hennecke-Schneemelcher, *NT Apocrypha*, i, (ET: London 1963), pp. 414 ff.

[13] Cf. Delling, *TWB*, v, pp. 824 ff.; J. M. Ford, *NTS* 12, (1966), pp. 293 ff.

will be free, and the captives delivered', are we to think of Luke 4.8? Or Romans 7.23? Or Ephesians 4.8? Does a contrast of slave and son, with a reference to inheritance in the context, necessarily imply a knowledge of Gal. 4.7? Finally, we must be careful about the conclusions we draw, for example with reference to the history of the Canon. Do such references and allusions, or even direct quotations, indicate that the books in question were already of canonical status, or merely that they were known and accorded a certain recognition? Are we justified in forming an estimate of the date of one of these documents and then, on the basis of this dating, drawing from the quotations in that document the conclusion that the development of the Canon was rather more rapid than was formerly believed; or should we argue conversely that the use of the New Testament, reflecting as it does a later stage in the development of the Canon, must be held to show that the document cannot be so early? When it comes to Textual Criticism, should we quote these texts as evidence for variant readings in New Testament passages, or as possible indications of the source of these variants? The Gospel of Thomas again is a case in point: if it is dependent on our Gospels, then its variants rank with the patristic quotations (with of course due regard to the possibility of tendentious modification) as evidence for the text of the Gospels in a particular area at a particular time; but if it is independent, then Thomas may itself have been the source of certain variants in the manuscript tradition. The problem is of course complicated by the further question of the relation between Thomas and the Diatessaron: which came first? Did Tatian use Thomas, or Thomas Tatian, or did both independently draw on the same older source?

To turn to specific instances, one example of the kind of thing that could happen is not precisely Gnostic, although it stands in the Gnostic tradition. Orosius says of Priscillian that he sought to establish his dualistic doctrine 'from a certain book entitled *Memoria Apostolorum,* wherein the Saviour appears to be questioned by the disciples in secret, and to show from the Gospel parable which has 'The sower went forth to sow' that he was not a good sower, asserting that if he had been good he would not have been neglectful, or cast seed 'by the wayside' or 'on stony places' or 'in untilled soil'; wishing it to be understood that the sower is he who scatters captive souls in diverse bodies as he wills.[14] Here the interpretation supplied in Mark is completely ignored, and the parable is interpreted in the light of Gnostic doctrine.

The parable of the Good Samaritan is quoted in the Gospel of Philip (111) in the context of a difficult passage, the point of which appears to be that the fragrance of a perfume is enjoyed not only by those who wear it but by others in their company, so long as the wearers are present. So the Gnostic imparts something of his own fragrance, but only so long as he is in this world. When he returns to the Pleroma, merely material men are left to their own evil odour. Then comes the reference: 'The Samaritan gave nothing to the wounded man except wine and oil. It is nothing other than the ointment. And he (or it?) healed the wounds. For love covereth a multitude of sins.' Here of course we may recall the allegorisation of the parable in Origen and Augustine;[15] but in Philip the wine and the oil are specifically identified with the ointment of the chrism. The prominence given in Philip to this sacrament, incidentally, sheds a new light on the references to a chrism in 1 John, although here again it is all too easy to read too much into the text.[16] The way in which the term is introduced in 1 John does suggest polemic against a false claim to the possession of a superior 'unction' on the part of the opposition; but we have no evidence at this stage for a sacrament with oil, such as was practised by the later Gnostic sects. On the other hand the metaphorical use of the term surely implies some reality which might serve as the basis for the metaphor. Another feature of the passage in Philip is of course the introduction of a verse from 1 Peter—one of those sayings which evidently became proverbial at an early stage, as they still are with us.

Such association and combination of texts drawn from diverse sources is characteristic. The Treatise on the Resurrection, for example, says:

[14] Hennecke-Schneemelcher, i, p. 266.

[15] Origen, *Hom. in Luc.*, xxxiv, [*GCS*, ix, p. 201 f.]; Augustine, *Quaest. Evang.*, ii.19; already in germ in Iren. *adv. haer.* 3.18.2 Harvey. Cf. Daniélou, *Origen*, (ET: London 1955), pp. 196 f., *Sacramentum Futuri*, (Paris 1950), pp. 246 f.

[16] Cf. Schnackenburg, *Die Johannesbriefe*, (Freiburg 1963), pp. 152 f.

As the Apostle said, we suffered with him and we arose with him, and we went to heaven with him.

(45.24–28)

Here the Apostle is manifestly Paul, the Apostle *par excellence* for the second century, but this is not an exact quotation; it is an amalgam of Pauline texts which, as it happens, implies the heresy refuted in the Pastorals, that the resurrection is already past.[17] In such cases it is sometimes exceptionally difficult to determine whether the writer is consciously selecting the material to suit his own purposes, giving a Pauline ring to what is actually Gnostic doctrine; or whether he is quoting loosely and from memory; or finally whether he is merely echoing the Pauline words and phrases, without any intention of accurately reproducing Paul's statements or his teaching. Anyone familiar with the Bible knows how readily its language springs to mind, offering an appropriate word or phrase, even in quite non-theological and even non-religious contexts; and it is clearly evident that many of the Gnostics were thoroughly steeped in the New Testament literature.

One of the more remarkable examples of this kind of association occurs in the Gospel of Thomas (log. 79):

A woman in the crowd said to him: Blessed is the womb which bore thee, and the breasts which nourished thee. He said to her: Blessed are they who have heard the word of the Father, and have kept it in truth. For there shall be days when you will say: Blessed is that womb which has not conceived, and those breasts which have not given suck.[18]

The first part of this logion has a parallel in Luke 11.27–28, but Thomas adds the words 'in truth' and substitutes 'which nourished thee' for 'which thou hast sucked'. The parallel to the second part is Luke 23.39, where as it happens some manuscripts read ἔθρεψαν, 'nourished', and others ἐθήλασαν, 'given suck'. There is room here for discussion as to the bearing of the readings in Thomas on the textual question in Luke: what is the significance of agreement between Thomas on the

---

[17] Cf. Rom. 8.17; Col. 3.1–4; Eph. 2.5–6 [see Malinine etc., *De Resurrectione*, (Zürich 1963), p. 27].

[18] See most recently W. Schrage, *Das Verhältnis des Thomas-Evangeliums zur synoptischen Tradition*, (Beiheft 29 zur *ZNW*, Berlin 1964), pp. 164 ff.

one hand and a whole series of witnesses to Luke on the other, including agreements at one point with the Sahidic version of Luke 23.29, at another with the Bohairic of Luke 11.27? A more important and indeed prior question is that of the relation between Thomas and Luke itself. The natural assumption is that Thomas drew upon Luke, but there is a danger here of assuming at the outset the very conclusion which has to be proved. Both the Lucan parallels belong to Luke's special tradition, so that we have no direct evidence for the form in which they came to Luke. In Thomas the passage as a whole fits so well together that it is legitimate to question whether *without the Lucan parallels* we should ever have suspected that the two parts did not originally belong together. We have therefore to reckon with the possibility that the passage was originally a unity, and raise the further questions: Is Thomas in fact combining two passages from Luke, or does this logion perhaps go back to tradition independent of Luke? Could it be that it was Luke who was responsible for the separation of the two parts, and not Thomas who combined them?

A decision here must rest upon what we can discover about the methods of the two authors. We know from comparison with Matthew that Luke generally adheres to the order of Q, keeping separate sayings which in Matthew are assembled together. Similarly, where Matthew tends to conflate Mark and Q, Luke keeps the material separate, resuming Mark's order again after introducing Q material. The implication is that it is Matthew's habit to conflate, whereas Luke retains the order of his sources. Only on the assumption that Luke used Matthew could it be argued that it was his practice to break up what was already combined, but against this assumption there are serious objections. On the other hand, there is in Thomas evidence in abundance for the compiler's tendency to combine material from different sources. Accordingly, the probability at this point favours the originality of Luke, but it should be noted (a) that it is a probability, and not an absolute certainty; the alternative, that it is Thomas who preserves the original form, remains at least a possibility; and (b) that conclusions drawn from this one saying are not necessarily valid for all the sayings in the Gospel of Thomas.

At the Crucifixion, according to the Gospels, 'the veil of the

Temple was rent in twain, from top to bottom.' In one apocryphal Gospel it is the lintel of the Temple which falls, but in
the Epistle to the Hebrews the rending of the veil is made the
basis of theological interpretation: it symbolises the free and
unhindered access to God achieved for all through the death of
Christ. Now the Gospel of Philip has two references to the veil.
The first unfortunately occurs in a badly damaged passage, and
all that we can really say is that the Gospel text is quoted, with
the words 'For it was fitting for some from below to go upward.'
The second passage however is extant in full:

> The veil at first concealed how God controlled the creation,
> but when the veil is rent and the things within are exposed
> this house will be left deserted, or rather will be [destroyed].
> But the whole deity will not flee [from] these places again into
> the holy of the holy [ones], for it will not be able to mix with
> the [unmixed light and] the [flawless] pleroma, but will be
> under the wings of the Cross [and under its] arms. This ark
> will be [for them] deliverance when the flood of water becomes
> powerful over them. If some are in the tribe of the priesthood,
> these will be able to go within the veil with the high priest.
> Because of this the veil was not rent at the top only, since it
> would be open only for those above; nor was it rent at the
> bottom only, since it would be revealed only to those below;
> but it was rent from top to bottom. Those above opened to us
> who are below, in order that we might go in to the secret of
> the truth . . .
>
> (Philip 125)

Here a whole speculation has been spun out of the apparently
quite subsidiary point that the veil was rent 'from top to
bottom'. The veil itself has become the firmament which separates the material world from the higher realms. The 'whole
deity' is the Demiurge with his powers, who cannot ascend into
the Pleroma but only to the region immediately beneath it,
separated from it by the barrier of the Cross—a feature of the
Valentinian system. As R. M. Grant has put it, 'This passage is
significant for Valentinian exegesis of the New Testament. It
shows that these Gnostics were busy at work combining various
New Testament passages, especially the more mysterious ones,
in an effort to produce new mysteries and fit them into their
system. It is also significant for the study of exegesis in general,

F

for it shows the dangers of allegorisation without the controls provided either by common sense or by some dogmatic system with roots on earth.'[19] It may be worth recalling the words of C. H. Dodd:[20] 'In the controversy with Gnosticism in the second and third centuries the main point at issue was whether the Christian faith could be detached from its biblical and historical basis and presented as a form of Hellenistic theosophy', or those of Bultmann:[21] 'Insofar as Christian preaching remained true to the tradition of the Old Testament and Judaism and of the earliest Church, *definitive contrasts between it and Gnosticism* are straightway apparent.'

In this passage of Philip, the 'house left desolate' comes from one passage of Matthew, 'destroyed' from another, 'under the wings' from a third; the ark recalls Hebrews 11.4 if we are thinking in terms of the Temple, but a more obvious reference is to the ark of Noah. Grant suggests that the author 'moves imaginatively from one ark to the other'. In any case we may refer to 1 Peter 3.20. Here, then, we have a whole series of New Testament texts woven together and pressed into the service of Valentinian theory.

Another example deals with the problem of the resurrection:[22]

Some are afraid lest they rise naked. Because of this they wish to rise in the flesh, and they do not know that those who bear the flesh [it is they who are] naked; those who . . . themselves to unclothe themselves [it is they who are] not naked. 'Flesh [and blood shall] not inherit the Kingdom [of God].' What is this which will not inherit? This which we have. But what is this which will inherit? That which belongs to Jesus with his blood. Because of this he said: He who shall not eat my flesh and drink my blood has no life in him. What is it? His flesh is the logos, and his blood is the Holy Spirit. He who has received these has food and drink and clothing. For myself, I find fault with the others who say that it will not rise. Then both of these are at fault. Thou sayest that the flesh will not

---

[19] *Journal of Biblical Literature* 79, (1960), p. 8. On the whole passage cf. Wilson, *The Gospel of Philip*, (London and New York 1962), pp. 190 ff.

[20] *According to the Scriptures*, (London 1952), pp. 136 f.

[21] *Theology of the NT*, i, (ET: London 1952), p. 168.

[22] Cf. J. Zandee, *Nederlands Theol. Tijdschr.* 16, pp. 361 ff.; Wilson, op. cit., pp. 87 ff.

rise; but tell me what will rise, that we may honour thee. Thou sayest the spirit in the flesh, and it is also this light in the flesh. But this too is a logos which is in the flesh, for whatever thou shalt say thou sayest nothing outside the flesh. It is necessary to rise in this flesh, in which everything exists.

(Philip 23)

At first sight, the author is frankly inconsistent here: first he denies the doctrine of the resurrection of the flesh, then he defends it. But when we compare the Treatise on the Resurrection and other parts of the Gospel of Philip it becomes plain that the situation is rather more complicated. A later passage (72) seems to make a distinction between the flesh of Jesus, which is 'true' flesh, and a flesh which is only an image of the true— which is a simple inversion of Paul's words in Romans about 'the likeness of sinful flesh'. The Letter of James in the Codex Jung makes Jesus say *after the Resurrection*: 'from now I shall unclothe myself in order that I may be clothed'. And there is a passage in the Ascension of Isaiah (9.9) in which the prophet sees 'Enoch and all who were with him' stripped of their earthly garments and arrayed in their heavenly robes, like the angels in glory.

It is commonly said that the Gnostics denied the resurrection of the flesh, on the ground that the flesh (being material) was evil and could have no part in the world of the spirit. This may be true of some Gnostics, but not for the group with which we are here concerned; or rather, while it is indeed *ultimately* true they introduced a further stage in the process. The idea here seems to be that the Gnostic must rise in the flesh, but only in order to be stripped of the garment of the flesh and put on his heavenly robe—in other words, they affirmed the Pauline doctrine but gave to it a twist of their own. In this case, the author of Philip first rejects the idea of a mere resurrection of the flesh, and then the 'Greek' conception that only the soul or spirit is immortal. In any event we have here allusions to three New Testament texts: 2 Cor. 5.3, 1 Cor. 15.50 and John 6.53 ff.—all once more pressed into the service of Gnostic theory. The exposition of the Johannine passage presents another feature of Gnostic exegesis in its identification of the flesh and blood there mentioned with the Logos and the Holy Spirit. That such methods were not confined to the Gnostics is shown by Ignatius, who identifies the flesh with faith and the blood with love (*Trall.* 8; cf. Ign. *Rom.* 7.3).

This passion for identification appears also in the Gnostic penchant for number-symbolism, neatly summarised by Turner:[23] 'The total number of Valentinian aeons is prefigured in the thirty years of the hidden life of our Lord and the total of the hours at which the labourers were called into the Vineyard. These divide into two groups of twelve and eighteen. The former are found in the number of disciples, the age at which our Lord paid His visit to the Temple, and the duration of the illness of the woman with the issue of blood. The Fall of Sophia corresponds with the Fall of the last disciple. The remaining group are represented in the eighteen months after the Resurrection during which, according to one tradition, our Lord taught Gnosis to his disciples. It is also the numerical value of the first two letters of the name of Jesus. Six was the number of evil and forty of the spiritual seed. Thus the forty-six years in which the Temple was built (John 2.20) bears the composite meaning of the indwelling of the spiritual seed in matter. The six husbands of the Samaritan woman also represent matter.' And so one could go on. There is justification for the comment of Henry Chadwick,[24] that the trouble with the Gnostics was not that they tried to apply reason to the Scriptures, but that they did not apply it enough. They are prone to allegory, but they can be literalists when it suits them, when a literal interpretation provides the means for adapting some scriptural passage to their own theories. Indeed, the distinction commonly drawn between literal and allegorical interpretation requires some modification here, for literalism and allegory can go hand in hand. The Gnostics often adhere to the literal *words* of Scripture, but have no regard for the literal *meaning* of the text as it stands. The words are accepted, but they are made to signify something quite different. The essential point is that it is the Gnostic theories which are dominant, and not the plain meaning of the Biblical text.

[23] *The Pattern of Christian Truth*, p. 236.

[24] In a lecture at St. Andrews. Cf. his *Early Christian Thought and the Classical Tradition*, (Oxford 1966), p. 9, and Brox, *Offenbarung, Gnosis u. gnostischer Mythos*, p. 17. The Gnostic texts often show a negative attitude to philosophy [cf. Quispel, *Gnosis als Weltreligion*, (Zürich 1951), pp. 23 f. and see further the texts discussed below].

Once again, however, it has to be noted that the Gnostics were not alone. Matthew, for example, frequently cites Old Testament passages the fulfilment of which he claims to find in New Testament events. The Epistle of Barnabas has a famous passage (9.8) in which the number of Abraham's servants in Gen. 14.14 is interpreted in terms of Jesus and the Cross (18 in Greek is *IH*, the first two letters of the name of Jesus; 300 is *T*, the symbol of the Cross). Philo of Alexandria devotes considerable attention to number symbolism, especially in relation to the numbers six, seven and ten; the first of these, incidentally, is given a very different interpretation from that of the Gnostics, for to Philo it is a perfect number (*Leg. alleg.* 1.3 ff.). It is not surprising that Gnostic exegesis provoked the early Fathers to exasperation, for the Gnostics were using the Church's books and employing the self-same methods of interpretation, but producing very different results.

In this connection it may be observed, as Barth already noted, that the Gnostics did not feel themselves bound to any one exegesis of any particular passage. On the Cry of Dereliction, for example, Barth notes that for the Gnostic it had on the lips of the Redeemer a blasphemous ring, and was therefore assigned to Sophia;[25] but the Gospel of Philip quotes it (72) with the express statement 'He said these words on the Cross'. Luke 1.35 appears to have been differently interpreted by Philip on the one hand (17; cf. 82) and the Excerpta ex Theodoto on the other (59–60). Barth draws a contrast between the ethical tension of Paul's words in Rom. 7.18 f. and the 'intellectualism' of John 8.32; but both these passages are echoed in Philip, and in the same context (Philip 123). And we have two divergent interpretations of the parable of the Lost Sheep. The Gospel of Truth finds an explanation in terms of number-symbolism:

> He is the Shepherd who abandoned the ninety-nine sheep which had not gone astray. He went in search of that one which had strayed. He rejoiced when he found it. For ninety-nine is a number which is in the left hand, which encompasses it. But as soon as the one is found the whole number passes over to the right. Thus it is with him who lacks the one, that is to say, the entire right hand, which attracts that which is

[25] *Die Interpretation des Neuen Testaments*, p. 68; cf. Wilson, *The Gospel of Philip*, p. 135.

lacking and takes it away from the left side, and passes over to the right; and in this way the number becomes a hundred.

(31.35 ff.)

In the Gospel of Thomas, however, we find:

> The Kingdom is like a shepherd who had a hundred sheep. One of them, the biggest, went astray. He left the ninety-nine and sought after the one till he found it. When he had laboured, he said to the sheep: I love thee more than the ninety-nine.

(log. 107)

It is at least open to question whether we ought to use the one to explain the other.

Another of the parables in Thomas is that of the treasure (log. 109):

> The Kingdom is like a man who had in his field a [hidden] treasure about which he did not know; and [after] he died he left it to his [son. The] son also did not know; he took (posses-son of) that field and sold it. The man who bought it came to plough, and [found] the treasure. He began to lend money at interest to whomsoever he chose.

The differences from Matthew's parable are considerable, and the whole point has been changed. In Matthew the treasure, like the pearl of great price, is something so precious that a man will go to any lengths to obtain it. Here in Thomas various explanations are possible: we may have the Gnostic classification of men into material, psychic and spiritual; or it may be that the man and his son represent Jews and Christians, who possess the treasure of Gnosis in the Scriptures without knowing it—only the Gnostic is able, in the words of the opening saying in Thomas, to find the interpretation of these words, hidden and secret words.[26] Or again the treasure, like the leaven or the grain of mustard-seed, may signify the divine self within man. Most men do not suspect what a treasure is laid up within them, and hence do not find 'the treasure in their field'; that is, they do not attain to a recognition of their true divine nature.[27] This

[26] A suggestion made by Dr. R. E. Taylor.

[27] Gärtner, *The Theology of the Gospel of Thomas*, (London 1961), p. 237; Haenchen, *Die Botschaft des Thomas-Evangeliums*, (Berlin 1961), p. 47; Schrage op. cit. [n. 18 above] pp. 196 ff.

third interpretation is supported by the fact that Hippolytus says the Naassenes identified the Kingdom with the treasure and the leaven (*Ref.* V.8.8) and with the mustard-seed (ibid. V.9.6); but this does not necessarily mean that other interpretations are either impossible or irrelevant. A further point is that a closer parallel than Matthew is to be found in a second-century Rabbinic text, and in one of Aesop's fables. The Gnostics here are elaborating their scriptural interpretation with the help of extraneous material.

The Gospel of Thomas, of course, presents the problem: is it or is it not Gnostic? It is perfectly possible to show how many of these mysterious sayings take on a meaning when they are translated into Gnostic terms, or rather interpreted in the light of our knowledge, from other sources, of Gnostic symbolism; but does this mean that this was their meaning from the outset? Was Thomas a Gnostic composition, or should we not reckon with the possibility that in its present form it is the result of a process of adaptation, and that much of the material originally had nothing to do with Gnosticism at all? Here we are confronted again with the problem which has already risen in connection with the New Testament: does the fact that a passage, or a document, can be read and understood in terms of Gnosticism mean that it is simply to be labelled Gnostic? To take but one example, the parable of the pearl:

> The Kingdom of the Father is like a merchant who had a load (of goods) and found a pearl. That merchant was wise. He sold the load, and bought for himself the pearl alone. You also, seek after his treasure which does not perish but endures, where moth does not enter to devour, nor does worm destroy.
>
> (log. 76)

Here again we have the combination of sayings from different passages, but the question for the present concerns the interpretation of the pearl.[28] In Matthew the pearl, like the treasure, is a symbol of the Kingdom, something of such surpassing value that a man will give up all he has to win it. But the Naassenes, interpreting the Matthaean saying about casting pearls before swine (Matt. 7.6, cf. Thomas 93), said that 'understanding and intelligences and men' (i.e. in Jonas' words, the 'living' elements

---

[28] Cf. above, pp. 19f.

in the physical cosmos) were 'the pearls of that Formless One cast into the formation (i.e. the body).' Later on in the Acts of Thomas, we have the famous Hymn of the Pearl, and in the Manichean Kephalaia there is an allegory which identifies the pearl with the soul. The question is: are we to interpret Thomas in terms of Matthew, or of the Manichean Kephalaia?

The Naassenes provide some justification for the latter procedure, the more especially in view of the parallels which have been noted; but here again we must ask: What is the significance of these parallels? Do they imply a Naassene origin for Thomas, or merely that the Naassenes used this document? It has been observed above that Hippolytus' account of the Naassenes seems to provide a clue to the understanding of some of these sayings. Grant and Freedman[29] note a number of similarities: 'significant examples of Gnostic interweaving' in the Naassene use of the Gospels, 'a tendency to combine words found in different contexts in order to bring out their Gnostic meaning.' Almost one might conclude that Thomas is a Naassene document, but Grant and Freedman merely say that the Naassenes knew and used Thomas, and that they 'quote several gospel sayings in a way which seems to reflect Thomas'. The point for their purpose is the similarity of method. More recently Haenchen[30] has given warning against an over-hasty association of Thomas with the Naassenes, affirming that it is *not* a Naassene gospel. There was of course nothing at all to prevent one school of Gnostics from using, quoting or adapting a document composed by another school, unless it was strictly reserved for members of the school of its origin; and we know that they did make use of 'orthodox' documents such as the New Testament writings themselves.

The point here is that it is by no means difficult to establish a table of correspondences: the robbers are the planetary powers who rule the destinies of men and hold the soul in subjection in the prison of the body; little children are the Gnostics; sleep and intoxication represent man's unregenerate state in this life, apart from the saving Gnosis, and so on. But we are left again and again with the question whether this table is in fact applicable in any given situation, whether for example it is even legitimate to apply it to the study of a New Testament text, to

[29] *The Secret Sayings of Jesus*, (London 1960), pp. 92 ff.
[30] *Botschaft*, p. 10.

the exclusion of what must seem the plain and natural meaning. To employ such a table of correspondences where it is not applicable is to find Gnosis and Gnosticism where none in fact exists, and to commit the very error of which the Gnostics themselves were guilty. Yet at times it is exceptionally difficult to be sure.

It was noted in the previous chapter that the references to the Gospels in Leisegang's index appear in most cases to relate to Gnostic re-interpretation of Gospel material. Basilides for example, according to Hippolytus,[31] says 'That everything has its own appointed seasons is sufficiently proved by the Saviour when he says "My hour is not yet come" (John 2.4), and by the Magi who saw the star (Matt. 2.1–2).' This of course is not specifically Gnostic; but a little earlier we have the passage:

The light which came down from the Ogdoad above to the son of the Hebdomad descended from the Hebdomad upon Jesus, the son of Mary, and he was enlightened, being set on fire by the light which shone into him. This is that which was spoken, 'Holy Spirit will come upon you', that which came down from the Sonship through the intermediate spirit upon the Ogdoad and the Hebdomad, as far as to Mary, 'and power of the Most High will overshadow you', the power of judgment from the height above through the demiurge as far as the creation, that which is of the son.[32]

This interpretation of Luke 1.35 does have some connection with the literal meaning of the verse, but it has been completely transposed into a Gnostic context and adapted to the needs of Basilides' system. A few lines further on there is an echo of Romans (8.19 and 22): the creation groans until now and is tormented and awaits the revelation of the sons of God, in order that all the men of the Sonship may ascend hence. Basilides evidently is weaving New Testament texts together into new patterns of his own design. Other examples of a similar kind may be found in abundance.

One point of some interest in this connection is that the same

---

[31] Hippol. *Ref.*, vii. 27.5 [Völker, *Quellen zur Geschichte der christlichen Gnosis*, (Tübingen 1932), p. 55].

[32] ibid., vii.26.8 f. [Völker, *Quellen*, p. 54]. For the use of Luke 1.35 cf. Philip 17 [Wilson, *The Gospel of Philip*, pp. 80 ff.], and *Exc. ex Theodoto* 59–60.

kind of use is made of Ephesians and Colossians. According to Ptolemy,[33] Christ on his return to the Pleroma was unwilling to descend a second time at the appeal of the abandoned Sophia, and sent the Paraclete, that is, the Saviour, 'the Father giving to him all power and handing over all under his authority, and the Aeons likewise, that "in him all things might be created, visible and invisible, thrones, deities, lordships",' (Col. 1.16). According to the Peratae,[34] 'the man Christ, who descended in the times of Herod, had a threefold nature, three bodies and three powers, since he contained in himself all the compounds and powers of the three parts of the cosmos. "And this is the meaning of the saying: He resolved that the whole fullness should dwell in him bodily, and that the whole Godhead should be in him" (Col. 2.9, cf. 1.19).' The Naassenes[35] in their exposition of the myth of Attis refer to the eternal essence 'where there is neither male nor female, but a new creation, a new man' (cf. Gal. 3.28, 6.15, 2 Cor. 5.17, Eph. 2.15, 4.24). As Leisegang puts it,[36] 'The motif of the castration of Attis is interpreted to mean that the originally bisexual Logos breaks apart within the Creation, and on earth through contact with matter is separated into a male and a female sex, only to be restored to heaven through the redemption of the male part alone. This motif is rediscovered in the Ephesians passages' (which are then quoted). It is evident from these examples that the New Testament material is here re-interpreted, sometimes with great ingenuity, to support some quite different kind of theory.

The point for present purposes is however that in these last instances we have Gnostic adaptation of passages from documents which are often claimed to have themselves been subject to the influence of Gnosticism. To argue that Paul, or his disciple, took such motifs from existing Gnostic theories which he did not understand and employed them for his own ends, and that the Gnostics later in apparently adapting Paul were in fact restoring the real and original meaning, is to make a whole series of assumptions for which there is no justification. On the contrary, the Gnostic adaptation of such passages must surely

---

[33] Ap. Iren. *Adv. haer.*, i.1.8 [Harvey 1, p. 38].
[34] Hippol. *Ref.*, v.12.5.
[35] Hippol. *Ref.*, v.7.15 [Völker, *Quellen*, p. 13].
[36] *Die Gnosis*, (Stuttgart 1955), p. 134.

be held to weaken the theory that such motifs were truly
Gnostic in the first place. At the very least these examples suggest the need for caution in the identification of Gnostic influence in the New Testament. The simplest and most obvious
explanation is that the Gnostics were using the New Testament
itself.

A more difficult question is whether it was the New Testament which was the basis for such speculations, or whether the
New Testament allusions, echoes and quotations are merely
secondary embellishment. There are cases in which a particular
motif appears to have developed out of speculation based on a
New Testament passage, but there are also cases where the New
Testament element can be removed from a document without
essential damage to its structure. A notable example is the
Naassene document,[37] where Reitzenstein separated a 'purely
pagan document' from the Christian commentary with which
it is interwoven; however, as Goppelt says, 'the Christian traits
prove to be later interpolation, but the Old Testament ones
cannot be detached', which may be a further pointer to a
Jewish form of Gnosticism lying behind the Christian. Other
examples are the Berlin Gospel of Mary, perhaps also the
Apocryphon of John, and also the Sophia Jesu Christi.[38] We can
therefore claim with some confidence the Christianisation of
certain texts, but whether these texts were originally not only
non-Christian but pre-Christian is another question.

Approaching this question from another angle, C. H. Dodd[39]
long ago pointed out that the Hermetic *Poimandres* shows no
dependence on Christian writings, although its thought does
have affinities with some aspects of early Christian thought, and
more particularly with Gnosticism. Indeed 'the Valentinian
system, apart from its definitely Christian elements, has the
aspect of an elaboration of a system very like that of the
Poimandres', and conversely the Poimandres 'has the aspect, not
of a simplification of something more elaborate, but of an

---

[37] Cf. Reitzenstein, *Poimandres*, (Leipzig 1904), pp. 81 ff., but see also
Burkitt in *JTS* 26 (1925) 117 ff.; L. Goppelt, *Christentum u. Judentum*,
(Gütersloh 1954), p. 134 [= *Jesus, Paul and Judaism*, (New York 1964),
p. 179].
[38] See chapter 5 below.
[39] *The Bible and the Greeks*, (London 1935), pp. 208–9.

experiment in the direction in which Valentinus travelled to a further stage.' The date of the Corpus Hermeticum is by no means certain, and in its present form the collection may be comparatively late, but some of the documents may date from the second Christian century and 'give the impression of being the deposit of many years of oral teaching, as well as of reflection and mystical meditation.'[40] If this be so, then the Hermetica would serve to show something of the kind of speculation current in certain circles already in the first century, and there would be full justification for Dodd's conclusion, that at an early stage in its career 'Christianity attracted the attention of thinkers who stood in the line of development of which the *Poimandres* is a representative', and who introduced the figure of Christ, with a varying measure of other Christian elements, into their speculations to produce the Gnostic systems.

It is no wonder that such fathers as Irenaeus waxed wroth with the Gnostics, for they were mishandling the Church's scriptures, and moreover they were doing so on principles and methods which the 'orthodox' themselves employed; for we can observe the use of the same methods and the same principles even in the works of the opponents of Gnosticism. The vital difference lay not so much in the methods as in the controlling factor: such a writer as Irenaeus is governed by the Church's Rule of Faith, whereas the Gnostics endeavour to mould the Scriptures to suit their own theories. The distinction is still relevant, and still merits consideration by exponents of modern theologies. There is all the difference in the world between an interpretation that is brought to the text from without and one which emerges from the text itself.

[40] C. K. Barrett, *The New Testament Background: Selected Documents*, (London 1956), p. 80.

IV

The New 'Gospels'

PRIOR to the publication of the Berlin Gnostic Codex by W. C. Till in 1955, our knowledge of Gnosticism was almost entirely based on the Christian refutations of the heresy by such Fathers as Irenaeus and Hippolytus, together with such extracts from Gnostic sources as they and other writers chose to quote: the excerpts from Theodotus among the writings of Clement of Alexandria, the fragments of Heracleon's commentary on the Fourth Gospel quoted by Origen, the letter of Ptolemy to Flora preserved by Epiphanius.[1] Since this material came through the hands of the opponents of Gnosticism, it was obviously open to some suspicion as the propaganda of the side which emerged victorious, deliberately selected to expose the weaknesses of Gnostic theory and to present the Gnostics themselves in the worst possible light. The only original Gnostic documents at our disposal were the three books of Pistis Sophia and an older unnamed work in the Askew Codex, and the two books of Jeu and another anonymous work in the Bruce Codex, all in Coptic and all dating from a period when Gnosticism was already in an advanced state of decline.[2] To these the Berlin Codex added another three, the Gospel of Mary, the Apocryphon of John, and the Sophia Jesu Christi.

It is this that gives the Nag Hammadi library its significance, for here we have more than forty different documents of various kinds, some of them in two or three copies, and presenting types of Gnosticism much nearer than the first group of texts above mentioned to those attacked by the Christian Fathers.[3] As A. D.

---

[1] *Excerpta ex Theodoto* ed. Casey, (London 1934), ed. Sagnard, (Paris 1948); *The Fragments of Heracleon* ed. Brooke, (Cambridge 1891), cf. Völker, *Quellen*, pp. 63 ff.; *Ptolemy to Flora* ed. Quispel, (Paris 1949).

[2] Cf. W. C. Till, *La Parola del Passato* 4, (1949), pp. 230 ff.

[3] Cf. Doresse, *The Secret Books of the Egyptian Gnostics*, (ET: London 1960). Bibliography to 1963 by S. Giversen in *Studia Theologica* 17, (1963), pp. 139 ff.

Nock wrote, 'The historical importance of this discovery may fairly be set on a level with that of the Dead Sea Scrolls. The latter throws new light on inter-testamental Judaism and on Christian beginnings; the former does something comparable for subsequent Christian development.'[4] To go no further, the texts so far published serve to confirm the conclusions reached through the researches of Foerster and Sagnard as to the essential reliability of Irenaeus, our earliest patristic authority.[5] Whatever its interest for the scholar, however, the Nag Hammadi discovery has not as yet attracted nearly the same public interest as the Scrolls, for reasons which are not far to seek. For one thing, the Gnostic texts have so far produced no sensation comparable to the suggestion that the Scrolls present the clue to the origins of Christianity, or even an anticipation of the faith itself. They belong quite definitely to the Christian era, and most of those so far published show very clear signs of Christian influence. For another, the records of a heresy long outmoded, a lost cause of a bygone age, cannot exert the same romantic appeal as the discovery of a whole field of thought and speculation hitherto unknown and well-nigh unsuspected; although Gnosticism too may have its lessons for the modern world. Again, the number of those who know Coptic, and hence can deal with these documents at first hand, is even smaller than in the case of Hebrew. And finally the publication of the texts has been beset by protracted and vexatious delays of one kind or another. The library was found in 1945 or 1946, but several years were to elapse before the main part of it finally passed into the possession of the Coptic Museum in Cairo. A photographic edition of some of this material was published in 1956, and translations of its contents were speedily made into German and later, in some cases, into other modern languages.[6] One codex meanwhile had been brought out of Egypt, and eventually found a resting place in the Jung Institute in Zürich. One of the

[4] *JTS* 9, (1958), p. 315.

[5] Foerster, *Von Valentin zu Heracleon*, (Beiheft 7 zur *ZNW*); Sagnard, *La gnose valentinienne*, (Paris 1947).

[6] P. Labib, *Coptic Gnostic Papyri in the Coptic Museum at Old Cairo*, (Cairo 1956); German translations in *TLZ* 1958–1959, most of them collected in Leipoldt-Schenke, *Koptisch-gnostische Schriften aus den Papyrus-Codices von Nag Hammadi*, (Hamburg-Bergstedt 1960).

documents it contains was published in 1957,[7] another in 1963.[8] The three Cairo texts of the Apocryphon of John appeared in 1962,[9] as did an anonymous treatise from Codex II,[10] and four apocalypses from Codex V in 1963.[11]

From one point of view it is regrettable that after the lapse of twenty years only thirteen documents, including the three in the Berlin Codex, have been adequately published out of more than forty, but the important thing is that progress is being made. Thirteen documents since 1955 represent a rather more favourable rate of progress than appears at first sight. After all, close on sixty years elapsed between the first announcement of the Berlin Codex and its eventual publication.[12]

It is commonly assumed that the collection was the library of a Gnostic group, and Doresse[13] suggests that it was hidden 'at the latest, about the beginning of the fifth century, at the time when the Pachomian monasteries . . . finally extended their influence over the region.' This is entirely plausible, but assumes the accuracy of the information supplied to Doresse regarding the location of the discovery. An alternative, suggested by T. Säve-Söderbergh,[14] is that the collection was made for heresiological purposes, in which case it may never have been owned as a whole by any single Gnostic group. This would materially affect our conclusions, for example as to the significance of the presence in the collection of a number of Hermetic texts, or of three versions of the Apocryphon of John; but in the present state of our knowledge it is impossible to decide. The strict orthodoxy of the Pachomian monks however suggests a reason for the concealment of the texts by a diminishing minority in the face of their growing influence, and the common view may therefore be allowed to stand.

[7] *Evangelium Veritatis*, ed. Malinine, Puech, Quispel, (dated Zürich 1956).

[8] *De Resurrectione*, ed. Malinine, Puech, Quispel, Till, (Zürich 1963).

[9] M. Krause and P. Labib, *Die drei Versionen des Apocryphon des Johannes*, (Wiesbaden 1962).

[10] A. Böhlig and P. Labib, *Die koptisch-gnostische Schrift ohne Titel aus Codex II von Nag Hammadi*, (Berlin 1962).

[11] Böhlig-Labib, *Koptisch-gnostische Apokalypsen aus Codex V von Nag Hammadi*, (Halle-Wittenberg 1963).

[12] W. C. Till, *Die gnostischen Schriften des koptischen Papyrus Berolinensis 8502*, (*TU* 60, Berlin 1955).

[13] *Secret Books*, p. 135.   [14] See his paper at the Messina Colloquium.

Of the documents so far available three, despite their differences, are sufficiently akin to be grouped together: the Gospel of Truth, the Gospel of Thomas and the Gospel of Philip. At least, they are all called 'Gospels'! Moreover all three have now been accessible long enough to allow of their intensive study, although it must be said that on some questions we are still a long way from any final conclusions. In particular, the publication of the remaining texts may yet entail considerable modification of prevailing opinions.

These three documents comprise in all some eighty pages of Coptic text. Even to present them in translation, without comment, interpretation or discussion, would require more than the space at our disposal; and as it happens each of them has had more than one complete book devoted to it. All that can be done here is to present a summary and even superficial outline of their contents and their significance, and of the problems they have helped to solve, or have themselves created.

It should be made clear at the outset, even at the present stage of research, that these documents are not 'Gospels' at all, in the sense in which this word is used as applying to the four canonical Gospels contained in our New Testament. They do not record the story of Jesus, nor do they give a connected account of his life and teaching, his death and resurrection. Two of them, the Gospel of Thomas and the Gospel of Philip, are so called because these are the names which are given to them in the manuscript in which they are contained. The third, the Gospel of Truth, owes its title to its opening words, and to the fact that Irenaeus in his refutation of the Gnostics speaks of a Gospel of Truth which was current among the Valentinians.[15] For this text begins 'The Gospel of Truth is joy for those who have received from the Father of Truth the grace of knowing Him.' It was but natural that the scholars who first examined the document should identify it with the treatise mentioned by Irenaeus, the more especially since it appears to be of a Valentinian character.

Formally the three texts are very different. The Gospel of Truth is a rather rambling treatise, aptly described as a meditation or homily on the theme of 'the Gospel', but for all its meandering it is a continuous text. Thomas on the other hand

---

[15] *Adv. haer.*, iii.11.12, [Harvey 2, p. 52].

is a collection of 'sayings' ascribed to Jesus, some very brief and others, especially the parables, of somewhat greater length, but all simply set down one after another with little apparent connection between them. Philip at first sight appears to be equally disjointed, but here there are some lengthy sections which cannot be properly classified as 'sayings', nor are they presented as sayings of Jesus. Moreover there are indications here that some of the units are linked by catch-words or by association of ideas, while another feature is the constant recurrence of a number of favourite themes.

The first of the three to appear was the Gospel of Truth, published in a very sumptuous edition dated 1956 and containing not only introduction, text, commentary and a full set of photographs but also French, German and English translations.[16] Four pages missing from the middle of the work were subsequently found among the Cairo fragments, and published in a supplementary volume.[17] An English translation with commentary was published by Kendrick Grobel in 1960, a French version with an attempt to put the text back into Greek by J. E. Ménard in 1962.[18] The latter also has a very comprehensive bibliography (pp. 21 ff.) for the Nag Hammadi library as a whole.

Publication of the text was anticipated by a number of articles and lectures, three of which were translated by F. L. Cross in the volume *The Jung Codex* (London 1955). In one of these W. C. van Unnik argues that the author was Valentinus himself, the founder of the Valentinian school, and that the work was written at Rome round about A.D. 140–145, before the development of the typically Gnostic dogmas. The main points of his argument are (a) the absence of 'the distinct and typical points of Valentinianism' in a document whose origin in the Valentinian circle is beyond question; (b) certain agreements with the surviving fragments of Valentinus; and (c) a certain reserve in the attitude of the document towards Docetism. In this opinion van Unnik has the general concurrence of Kendrick

---

[16] See n. 7 above.

[17] *Evangelium Veritatis* (Supplementum), ed. Malinine etc., (Zürich and Stuttgart 1961).

[18] Grobel, *The Gospel of Truth. A Valentinian Meditation on the Gospel*, (London 1960); Ménard, *L'Evangile de Vérité*, (Paris 1962).

G

Grobel and of R. M. Grant,[19] although they do not agree on points of detail; but the editors of the published edition, although they mention the theory with respect, are prepared to go no further than to say that the composition of the document may go back to about A.D. 150, and that the author may have been Valentinus or one of his immediate disciples.

The factors underlying the more general ascription of the document to the Valentinian school are (a) that with one possible exception all the texts included in this particular codex appear to be Valentinian, and (b) that the document itself shows agreement in language and in doctrine with the Valentinian system. It refers to aeons, to the Pleroma, to the place of rest, to the classification of mankind into spiritual, psychic and material, and so on—all terms familiar from the accounts of Valentinianism given by Irenaeus and other early Fathers. But the author makes a quite unique use of these terms, and his teaching as a whole does not coincide with any known form of Valentinianism. In particular there is no detailed list of the aeons, no account of the way in which they emanated from the primal deity; there is no myth of the fall of Sophia, so prominent in the Valentinian doctrine as previously known; and there is no mention of the Demiurge, or of the distinction between him and the supreme God.

This general 'Valentinian' ascription has been challenged from different angles. H. M. Schenke[20] claimed that the Gospel of Truth shows nothing specifically Valentinian at all, and that its central ideas are more akin to those of the Odes of Solomon; but the origins and associations of these Odes are themselves disputed, and when they were first published they were claimed by many scholars as Valentinian! Ernst Haenchen,[21] again, declared that the differences between the Gospel and Valentinianism were such that to pass from one to the other consti-

[19] Grant, *Gnosticism and Early Christianity*, (New York and London 1959), pp. 128 ff. Cf. also the discussion by H. C. Puech in Hennecke-Schneemelcher, *NT Apocrypha*, i, pp. 233 ff.

[20] *Die Herkunft des so-genannten Evangelium Veritatis*, (Berlin 1958). Links with the Odes of Solomon were also noted by F. M. Braun, *Rev. Thomiste* 57, (1957), pp. 597 ff. [cf. his *Jean le Théologien*, (Paris 1959), pp. 235 ff.], and R. M. Grant, *Vig. Chr.* 11, (1957), pp. 149 ff.

[21] *ZKG* 67, (1955–56), p. 154; cf. also his survey in *ThR* 30, (1964), pp. 47 ff.

tuted a *metabasis eis allo genos*; but this is to ignore the possibility of growth and development within the Valentinian system. For example, the suggestion has been made, though never fully explored, that the Gospel of Truth represents a primitive stage, and that the developed Valentinianism known to Irenaeus results from the subsequent assimilation of some such theory as that represented by the Apocryphon of John. It must be remembered that what we have in Irenaeus is not the system of Valentinus himself but that of his disciples—and their disciples.

At this point attention should be drawn to the ambiguity of the term 'Valentinian' in this connection, for it is not always clear whether it should be taken to refer to Valentinus himself or to his school. Some scholars would be prepared to accept a Valentinian origin in the latter sense but not, with van Unnik, in the former. Again, due heed should be paid to Haenchen's warning[22] against hasty ascription of authorship. Much as we should like to identify the authors of our documents, and greatly as it would simplify our task, the fact remains that often we simply do not know, nor have we any adequate basis for making such identifications. As it is, Valentinus has been credited with the authorship both of the Gospel of Truth and of the Epistle to Rheginus, and more recently Mademoiselle Pétrement[23] has suggested that he may also be the author of the Epistle to Diognetus, or part of it. The arguments advanced in such cases may carry considerable weight, but they must always be received with a due measure of reserve.

A third challenge is that of Hans Jonas,[24] who argues that the Gospel of Truth does not ante-date but presupposes the developed Valentinian system, that in other words it does not mention the missing elements just because they are taken for granted. This question is important because upon it depends our estimate of the place of this Gospel in the development of Valentinianism. If van Unnik is correct, we can trace something of the growth of the theory, in particular a movement away from Christianity—which would serve to confirm, so far as the Valentinians are concerned, the traditional view of Gnosticism

---

[22] *ThR* 30, (1964), p. 57.

[23] *Rev. Hist. Phil. Rel.*, (1966), pp. 34 ff.

[24] Cf. his review in *Gnomon* 32, (1960), pp. 327 ff., also *Studia Patristica*, vi, (Berlin 1962), pp. 96 ff.

as a Christian heresy; and moreover we should be able to identify one at least of the influences which were operative, namely the Barbelognostic system described by Irenaeus and now more fully available in the Coptic Apocryphon of John. On the other hand, if Jonas is right we have to assume that the full Valentinian system is already present behind even so comparatively early a document as the Gospel of Truth. In point of fact it is not difficult to extract from it numerous passages which fit neatly into the system described by Irenaeus, but *does* this mean that the whole system was already present? Or was the Gospel perhaps the work of some unknown Valentinian, who sought to work out a closer rapprochement with Christian doctrine? Here obviously much remains to be done.

In regard to the character of the document, Puech and Quispel in their pioneer article regarded it as a fifth Gospel, intended to supplement or supersede the canonical form, but they themselves subsequently accepted van Unnik's argument, now generally adopted, that it is rather a meditation on the theme of the Gospel, 'a sermon, a devotional contemplation, or, if one will, a dogmatic or mystical tractate.'[25] Some Scandinavian scholars would be even more specific and claim it as a baptismal or confirmation homily, and in this they are followed by Sasagu Arai, a Japanese scholar whose well-documented study of the Christology of the Gospel of Truth represents the latest contribution to research on this text.[26] Baptismal elements are certainly present but, as in the more familiar case of 1 Peter, not every scholar is quite confident that we have to do with a baptismal homily.

Since 1959 this text has been rather overshadowed by the Gospel of Thomas.[27] This is only natural, in view of the charac-

[25] Puech-Quispel, *Vig. Chr.* 8, (1954), pp. 22 ff.; van Unnik in *The Jung Codex*, p. 95 [cf. p. 106 n. 1].

[26] T. Säve-Söderbergh, *RoB* 17, (1958), cited by Segelberg, thinks it a baptismal homily. E. Segelberg (*Orientalia Suecana*, Uppsala 1960; cf. *Studia Patristica*, v, (Berlin 1962), pp. 118 ff.) calls it rather a confirmation homily, and stresses not the kinship but the differences between it and the Odes of Solomon. See also S. Arai, *Die Christologie des Evangelium Veritatis*, (Leiden 1964), p. 14.

[27] First published in P. Labib's photographic edition, *Coptic Gnostic Papyri in the Coptic Museum at Old Cairo*, (Cairo 1956), and subsequently the subject of a very extensive literature. For the earlier studies, cf. Puech in Hennecke-Schneemelcher, i, pp. 278 ff.

ter of the latter document: a collection of sayings, some of them
parallel to sayings already familiar, others entirely new; and
more particularly because of the possible significance of this
collection for the development of the early Gospel tradition. Yet
the Gospel of Truth is a more comprehensible document. It has
of course its difficulties and obscurities, and the author mean-
ders, turning his theme about and approaching it now from one
angle, now from another. But there is some continuity in his
meandering, whereas in Thomas there seems to be nothing of
the sort. On the contrary, sayings and parables which in our
Gospels appear in the same context are in Thomas widely
separated, or are brought into association with other sayings
from completely different contexts. Familiar sayings appear in
unfamiliar forms and unfamiliar groupings, while others again
have no canonical parallels but are cited by early Fathers as
occurring in the Gospel of the Hebrews or the Gospel of the
Egyptians; and still others are entirely new.

Phenomena such as these inevitably give rise to questions:
What is the relation between Thomas and our Gospels—is it
dependent on them, or independent? What is its background,
its origin, what are its sources? Here as so often we are confronted by problems of method and approach. There are at
least two distinct approaches, which lead to two divergent
results.[28] On the one hand there are those scholars who begin
with the question of the relation of Thomas to the Synoptics,
and who may or may not conclude that it is largely independent.
On the other hand an approach from the angle of theology,
from the point of view of an analysis of the doctrine which the
document contains, leads on the whole to the conclusion that it
is a Gnostic text, and secondary to our Gospels.[29] Now there is no
question that we can put a Gnostic theology into Thomas, that
if we approach it with Gnostic theory in mind we can find a
meaning for much that is otherwise obscure. But is this the whole
answer?[30] Or are we not once more faced by the danger of

[28] E. Haenchen, *Die Botschaft des Thomas-Evangeliums*, (Berlin 1961), pp.
37 f., makes a similar but slightly different distinction in relation to the
interpretation of the document.

[29] Cf. Haenchen, op. cit.; B. Gärtner, *The Theology of the Gospel of Thomas*,
(London and New York 1961).

[30] Cf. for example K. Grobel in *NTS* 8, (1962), pp. 367 ff., and on the
other side Y. Janssens, *Le Muséon* 75, (1962), pp. 301 ff.

imposing on the text a preconceived interpretation? Granted that the gospel as it now stands can be read as a Gnostic document, does this mean that it was Gnostic from the first, that it was composed by a Gnostic and with the full Gnostic theory present to his mind? Or should we not consider, here as in other respects, the possibility of growth, the possibility that a document originally non-Gnostic has been taken over, adapted and embellished, to serve a Gnostic purpose?[31]

Broadly speaking, the earlier studies on Thomas all tended to favour some degree of independence from our Gospels, but the more recent trend has been towards the view that Thomas used the canonical books.[32] The first book published in English on the subject, by R. M. Grant with David Noel Freedman, does indeed touch on the possibility of independent tradition, but no more. The evidence provided by Papias, they say, is not such as to inspire confidence in the reliability of the oral tradition in that period—in fact 'we may wonder whether oral tradition, by his time, was not getting rather garbled.'[33] So they conclude (p. 102) that while Thomas *may* have used traditions underlying our Gospels it is more likely, if he wrote towards the middle of the second century, that he relied on written documents.

The chief protagonist of the theory of independence has been G. Quispel, although a somewhat similar theory has also been advanced by Oscar Cullmann.[34] Starting from the fact that one logion in Thomas is quoted by Clement of Alexandria as from the Gospel of the Hebrews, and that others show affinities with citations from the Gospel of the Egyptians, Quispel argues that these were the original sources which Thomas drew, and goes on to trace the influence of this independent tradition in

[31] Thus G. Quispel argues [e.g. in *The Bible in Modern Scholarship*, (Nashville 1965), pp. 256 f.] that Thomas is not Gnostic but Encratite.

[32] For details see R. McL. Wilson, *Studies in the Gospel of Thomas*, (London 1960), where full references are given to the earlier literature.

[33] Grant and Freedman, *The Secret Sayings of Jesus*, (London 1960), p. 26. A somewhat different picture of the survival of oral tradition emerges from Helmut Köster's *Synoptische Überlieferung bei den apostolischen Vätern*, (*TU* 65, Berlin 1957).

[34] Quispel's earlier papers are listed in my *Studies in the Gospel of Thomas*. Cf. more recently by the paper cited in n. 31. Cullmann's articles appeared in *TLZ*, (1960), cols. 321 ff. [ET: in *Interpretation* 16, (1962), pp. 418 ff.; cf. also *Universitas* 4, (1961), pp. 141 ff., *Hibbert Journal* 60, (1961), pp. 116 ff.].

the Diatessaron of Tatian, in the pseudo-Clementines, and elsewhere in early Christian literature. Not all his arguments are
equally cogent, and some may be considered frankly weak. In
particular there is the difficulty that we possess so little either of
the Gospel of the Hebrews or of the Gospel of the Egyptians,
which makes any far-reaching conclusions relating to either
precarious in the extreme. Nevertheless, the case is not one to be
lightly swept aside without more ado. Could it but be substan-
tiated in detail, it would shed fresh light on the whole development of early Christianity, particularly in Syria.[35]

On the positive side, one thing is certain, that Thomas
includes all the sayings contained in the three famous Oxyrhynchus Logia papyri. Even here however there are differences
which make it dangerous to assume that the papyri present the
original Greek from which the Coptic Thomas was translated.
One saying in POx.1 is in Thomas divided into two, with some
forty other logia between. We therefore have to reckon with the
possibility of development between the Greek fragments in the
third century and the Coptic Gospel in the fourth or fifth; and
once this is granted it becomes necessary to enquire whether
such development may not also have taken place even earlier.
It is not difficult to imagine, although it would be very difficult
to prove, a process in which some elements were taken from the
oral tradition (sometimes at a later stage than that represented
in our Gospels), while others are in some measure dependent on
the canonical books, and others again are purely 'Gnostic' or at
least Encratite constructions. In such a case, proof of the
dependence of any given saying would have no significance for
any other saying; each would require to be considered on its own
merits.

The latest contribution here, by W. Schrage,[36] sets out the
Coptic text of the relevant sayings with the Sahidic version of

[35] Support for some of Quispel's views is provided by A. Baker, *Vig. Chr.*
18, (1964), pp. 215 ff. [cf. Quispel ibid., 226 ff.]; *JTS* 16, (1965), pp.
449 ff.; *NTS* 12, (1965), pp. 49 ff. On the other hand his attempt to link
Thomas with the Anglo-Saxon *Heliand* has met with determined resistance,
from the side of *Germanistik*, from W. Krogmann [see most recently *Vig. Chr.*
18, (1964), pp. 65 ff.].

[36] W. Schrage, *Das Verhältnis des Thomas-Evangeliums zur synoptischen
Tradition und zu den koptischen Evangelienübersetzungen*, (Beiheft 29 zur *ZNW*,
Berlin 1964). Cf. my review in *Vig. Chr.* 20, (1966), pp. 118 ff.

the Synoptic parallels below. Schrage claims that Thomas
shows not only a knowledge of our Gospels, but also an astonish-
ing familiarity with the Coptic versions thereof. This might
seem decisive, but unfortunately he proves too much; for
Thomas shows agreements not only with the Sahidic but with
the Bohairic, sometimes separately and in the same saying;
elsewhere he is actually closer to the Greek than the Coptic
versions are. Nor has Schrage taken sufficient account of the
question how far the words used in common were the obvious
and even the inevitable words for a translator to employ.
Moreover there are a few logia for which no parallels are
supplied because the differences are too great. Evidently the
problem is more complex than appears at first sight, and much
still remains to be done.

The Gospel of Philip is still something of an enigma. For one
thing it is only recently that the Coptic text has been made
available in convenient form, or an English translation provided, although we have had a German version for some years
past.[37] We are still at the stage of clarifying, explaining and
emending obscure passages in the text, and collecting the necessary parallels and comparative material.[38] Nor is it clear what
should be said as to the character of this document. H. M.
Schenke, who did the pioneer work, described it as a kind of
Gnostic florilegium, and divided it into 127 'Sprüche'. But here
already we must pause for reflection: was he perhaps unduly
influenced by the example of Thomas? Some of these 'sayings',
even on Schenke's division, are extremely long, and there are
cases where he seems to have put asunder what was originally

[37] First published in Labib's photographic edition (see n. 6). German
version by H. M. Schenke in *TLZ* 1959, reprinted in Leipoldt-Schenke,
Koptisch-gnostische Schriften aus den Papyrus-Codices von Nag-Hammadi, (Hamburg-Bergstedt 1960), pp. 33–65 and 81 f. English translation by C. J. de
Catanzaro, *JTS* 13, (1962) pp. 35 ff. and (independently, with commentary)
by R. McL. Wilson, *The Gospel of Philip*, (London and New York 1962).
Text with German translation by W. C. Till, *Das Evangelium nach Philippos*,
(Berlin 1963).
[38] Cf. J. W. B. Barns' review of Wilson in *JTS* 14, (1963), pp. 496 ff.,
and M. Krause's review of Till in *ZKG* 75, (1964), pp. 168 ff., the latter
based on more adequate photographs than those available to earlier
contributors. See also A. Helmbold, *NTS* 11, (1964/5), pp. 90 ff., and
W. C. van Unnik, ibid., 10, (1963/4), pp. 465 ff.

joined.[39] The most recent editor, J. E. Ménard, takes a different line.[40] Noting that some of these sections appear to be linked by catchwords, he suggests that this is the clue to the continuity and progression of the thought, and that sometimes we should take two or even three of Schenke's sections together. But Ménard himself cannot carry the process through from beginning to end of the work. If this is the Ariadne thread to guide us through the labyrinth, there are places where it has been broken.

If the structure and plan of the book are still obscure, its Gnostic character is beyond dispute. It is definitely and unambiguously a Gnostic work, nor does it raise any such interesting and attractive theories as does Thomas, with the possibility of independent tradition lying behind it. The question here is one of fitting it into its proper place in the development of Gnosticism. There are clear links with the Valentinian theory, in particular with the Marcosian version as described by Irenaeus, and with the Excerpta ex Theodoto of Clement of Alexandria. In fact there are passages which can only be understood in the light of what Irenaeus tells us; but curiously there are others where the closest parallels are to be found not in Irenaeus' discussion of Gnostic theories but in his own Demonstration of the Christian faith. This is a reminder that the Gnostics were not always so far removed from 'orthodox' Christianity. In the early stages especially there was a good deal of common ground, and it was only gradually that the lines of division emerged.

One point of special interest is the considerable number of allusions, tantalising in that they are only allusions and not full descriptions, to Gnostic sacraments. Baptism and the Eucharist of course are shared with the Great Church, but there are references also to the Chrism, which for the author ranks as superior to Baptism; to the Apolutrosis which appears to be characteristic of the Marcosians, and finally to one which appears to rank above them all but is never precisely defined: the bridal chamber. We know the Valentinians gave a special place to marriage, regarding human marriage as symbolic of the union of the aeons in the heavenly realm; but is it to marriage that Philip refers, or to some ceremony akin to the 'sacred

[39] In a survey of research published in *TLZ* 90, (1965), cols. 321 ff., Schenke now adopts the more general term 'paragraph'.

[40] J. E. Ménard, *L'Evangile selon Philippe*, (Montreal and Paris 1964).

marriage' of which we read in connection with some ancient religions of the Middle East?

Another point of interest in this document is its use of the New Testament, whether by direct quotation or in its Gnostic interpretation of New Testament themes and ideas.[41] Here a word of warning is required: it is all very well to list the references and allusions, but what do they signify for the history of the Canon? Full canonicity, or merely knowledge of the books in question? For example, van Unnik argued from the Gospel of Truth that almost the whole of our New Testament was already recognised as authoritative in Rome by about A.D. 150, but the argument could be reversed: the stage of development here reflected might be claimed to show that this document cannot possibly be so early. The dates of all these documents, it must be said, are still rather conjectural. Van Unnik dates the Gospel of Truth about A.D. 140–145, Grobel and Grant slightly later. If Jonas is right, it may be perhaps a generation later, which might agree better with the state of the Canon here reflected. Puech puts the earliest redaction of Thomas about A.D. 140, but the problem here is very complex, since we have to allow for the possibility of growth. The Oxyrhynchus Logia are dated between A.D. 200 and 250, but are they fragments of Thomas, or were they later incorporated into it? Or are the Logia on the one hand and Thomas on the other both versions of some earlier document? Again, if Thomas is dependent on Tatian, this provides a *terminus a quo*; but if Tatian is dependent on Thomas it is a *terminus ante quem*. The closest affinities of Philip appear to be with the Marcosians and the Excerpta ex Theodoto, which would put this document near the time of Irenaeus (*c.* A.D. 170–180). Ménard lists a number of themes which can be found in the later forms of Gnosis: in Mandeism, the Pistis Sophia and Manicheism. He accordingly places the origin of Philip in this milieu, and takes the third century as the *terminus a quo* for this document. The question is however whether Philip presupposes the doctrines of such groups, as Ménard seems to assume, or anticipates them. At all events, we can hardly put this gospel before the final quarter of the second century or the beginning of the third. Nor do the three texts provide any adequate basis for constructing a relative chrono-

[41] Cf. R. McL. Wilson, *NTS* 9, (1963), pp. 291 ff.

logy. Mademoiselle Y. Janssens[42] has recently suggested that Philip and Thomas derive from different, although perhaps parallel, currents of thought, and hence it is impossible to say which is the older, since they do not follow the same line. The same would appear to be true of the Gospel of Truth: unless it is by Valentinus himself, in which case it is certainly the oldest of the three, we have no real basis for determining whether it is older than the other two or not.

One passage in particular in Philip is of interest as showing how a Gnostic could take over and adapt Paul's teaching on the resurrection[43]—which may help to explain Tertullian's emphasis on resurrection not only of the body but of the flesh; for Paul's doctrine may have served Gnostic interests all too well. Another passage presents a curious and, so far as yet known, unique piece of speculation about the Cross:

> Philip the apostle said 'Joseph the carpenter planted a garden because he needed the wood for his trade. It was he who made the Cross from the trees which he planted. And his seed hung on that which he planted. His seed was Jesus, but the planting was the Cross.'

> (Philip 91)

Finally, there is the contribution which this text can make to the study of Gnostic imagery and symbolism.

This review is of course very far from being exhaustive—a recent survey on Thomas alone lists ninety titles[44]—but it may serve to give some indication of the progress made, the problems encountered, and the tasks remaining.

[42] *Byzantion* 35, (1965), p. 454.
[43] Philip 23 [see above, pp. 74 ff.].
[44] H. Quecke, in *La Venue du Messie*, (1962), pp. 271 ff.

V

The other Published Documents from Nag Hammadi

SOME twelve years ago our materials for the study of Gnosticism proper consisted almost entirely of the Christian refutations, with such fragments of original Gnostic documents as they contain, and a handful of original texts preserved in Coptic, all of them comparatively late. The Berlin Coptic papyrus had long been known, and had indeed to some extent been utilised, but only in the autumn of 1955 was it finally published, thus making three further texts available: the Gospel of Mary, the Apocryphon of John, and the Sophia Jesu Christi. Since then nine of the Nag Hammadi documents have been published in text and translation, with commentaries more or less detailed and comprehensive: the three Gnostic gospels discussed in the previous chapter, the Treatise on the Resurrection (otherwise known as the Epistle to Rheginus), four Gnostic apocalypses, and the anonymous treatise contained in Codex II. In addition the three Nag Hammadi versions of the Apocryphon of John, which vary at sundry times and in divers manners from the Berlin text, are now at our disposal, and the Hypostasis of the Archons has been translated into German.

The primary concern of the present chapter is with the eight remaining Nag Hammadi documents in the above list. The library however contains copies not only of the Apocryphon of John but also of the Sophia Jesu Christi and of a related document, which were used by Dr. Till in his edition of the Berlin text, and it therefore seems appropriate to include some discussion of these also, and of the relevant problems, even though the Nag Hammadi copies have not yet appeared. It is then rather pointless to omit the comparatively short Gospel of Mary, even though it does not strictly belong to the new discovery. With this accordingly we begin.

1. *The Gospel of Mary (Berlin Codex)*.[1] This is the first of the three texts in the Berlin Codex, but six pages are missing at the beginning and a further four later on (pp. 11–14), so that of the original eighteen pages little more than eight remain. The final pages are extant in Greek in a papyrus in the John Rylands collection in Manchester.[2] The document falls into two distinct parts, of which the first is a conversation between the Saviour and his disciples. It begins in the middle of a question about the destiny of matter, to which the Saviour replies 'All natures, all formations, all created things exist in and with one another and will again be resolved into their own roots. For the nature of matter is dissolved into the roots of its nature alone.' Peter then asks 'What is the sin of the world?', and receives the reply 'There is no sin, but it is you who make sin when you do what is of the nature of fornication, which is called "sin".' Then follows a brief farewell address, composed largely of a tissue of New Testament quotations and allusions, and the Saviour takes his departure. At this the disciples are plunged into despair, but they are comforted and encouraged by Mary.

Here one might expect the document to end, but in fact it continues with a request from Peter to Mary, that she impart to them the revelations given to her by the Saviour, which she therefore knows and they do not. The reply is interrupted by the four-page lacuna already mentioned, but includes an account of a vision and, after the lacuna, part of a description of the ascent of a soul and its conversations with a succession of hostile powers. Andrew however bluntly expresses his disbelief, and is supported by Peter, and at this Mary is reduced to despair. Levi comes to her defence, and wins over the others. The text ends with the statement that they 'began to go out to preach and proclaim'.

As Puech observes,[3] there is a contrast between the dominant role which Mary plays in the second part of the work and the modest place which she assumes in the first, and this together

---

[1] Text in Till, *TU* 60, pp. 62 ff.; English translation in Grant, *Gnosticism. An Anthology*, (London 1961), pp. 65 ff. See also Puech in Hennecke-Schneemelcher, i, pp. 340 ff.

[2] C. H. Roberts, *Catalogue of the Greek and Latin Papyri in the John Rylands Library*, iii, (Manchester 1938), pp. 18 ff. [P Ryl. 463].

[3] op. cit., p. 344.

with the diversity of the content suggests that two originally independent documents have been artificially combined. This conclusion, also drawn by Till, appears to be confirmed by the fact that the New Testament allusions almost all occur either at the beginning or in the suture between the two parts.[4] The second part, however, forms a fairly coherent whole, and it is difficult to believe it the result of a redaction which consisted only in the substitution of New Testament names for those in the original document. Consideration must therefore be given to the possibility that we have here not the combination of two earlier *documents* but a Christian Gnostic composition into which earlier and non-Christian material has been incorporated. At all events, we do seem to have in this document evidence of the Christian Gnostic redaction of older material, although it should be added that even if this material was non-Christian it was not necessarily also *pre*-Christian. The age and character of this material still requires to be examined.

Another point of interest is the opposition encountered by Mary from the side of Andrew and Peter. As Puech notes,[5] this has its parallels in the Pistis Sophia, and more particularly in the Gospel of Thomas (log. 114). Mary Magdalene of course occupies a privileged position in Gnostic literature (cf. also Philip 32, 55), but what are we to make of Peter's hostility? Is it merely an echo, or a development, of the unbelief with which, according to our Gospels (Mark 16.11, Luke 24.11), the disciples greeted the news of the Resurrection,[6] or is there another significance? The Church of Rome, as Kelly puts it, 'regarded itself and was regarded by many, as in a special sense the appointed custodian and mouthpiece of the apostolic tradition.'[7] When Irenaeus seeks to defend the authentic apostolic doctrine against Gnostic innovations, it is to the tradition of Rome that he appeals, the church founded by Peter and Paul (*adv. haer.* III.3.1 Harvey). Is Peter then in the Gnostic gospels representative of the church of Rome? The suggestion is certainly

---

[4] Cf. *NTS* 3, (1957), pp. 233 ff.

[5] op. cit., p. 343.

[6] Cf. the *Epistula Apostolorum* 10 ff. [Hennecke-Schneemelcher, i, pp. 195 ff.]

[7] *Early Christian Doctrines*, (London 1958), p. 44. Cf. R. P. C. Hanson, *Tradition in the Early Church*, (London 1962), pp. 144 ff.

attractive, but it may also be misleading. At what stage, for example, did Peter become so identified with the Roman church that he could stand as its representative? Or would such an interpretation not involve a rather later period for these Gnostic documents than the second-century date hitherto suggested? Such questions call for further and more detailed investigation. As Hanson notes,[8] Irenaeus (unlike Cyprian later) 'consistently speaks of both Peter and Paul as founding the Roman church and never connects the importance of the Roman church with our Lord's words to Peter recorded in the gospels.'

2. *The Apocryphon of John.*[9] In the Berlin Codex the Apocryphon of John follows immediately on the Gospel of Mary. Indeed Carl Schmidt at first thought they formed a single document, a mistake which he later corrected but which is still occasionally perpetuated by those who have not consulted either his later writings or the published edition of the Codex. In addition, we now have no fewer than three copies in the Nag Hammadi library,[10] one of them close to the Berlin text and collated by Dr. Till for his edition, the others rather longer, although one of them unfortunately is in a somewhat fragmentary condition.

Part of the interest in this document lies in the fact that the first section, containing the account of the origin of the world, tallies very closely with the account of the Barbelognostics given by Irenaeus (*adv. haer.* I.27 Harvey) and that, as Sagnard notes,[11] we are here touching upon the sources of the Valentinian Gnosis. Schmidt[12] many years ago claimed this document as the source of Irenaeus' account, arguing that the original used by Irenaeus extended beyond his excerpt. In the following chapter Irenaeus presents in detail an extract from another source, which overlaps with the material in the Apocryphon. Hence he breaks off where he does simply to avoid repetition.

[8] op. cit., p. 145.

[9] Text in Till, pp. 78 ff.; English translation in Grant, *Anthology*, pp. 69 ff. See also Puech in Hennecke-Schneemelcher, i, pp. 314 ff.

[10] Cf. Krause-Labib, *Die drei Versionen des Apocryphon des Johannes*. The Codex II version has been published with an English translation by S. Giversen, *Apocryphon Johannis*, (Copenhagen 1963).

[11] *La gnose valentinienne*, pp. 445 f.

[12] In *Philotesia*, (Berlin 1907), pp. 317 ff.

On this view we should have to date the Apocryphon at any rate before A.D. 180.

The situation now, however, is rather less simple. We now have four versions, two short and closely similar and two rather longer. We therefore have to ask which of them is the older, the 'long recension' or the short, and what is their relation one to another, before we can go on to examine the relationship between them and Irenaeus. Is the long recension the original, or is it an expansion of the shorter? Did Irenaeus know the longer or the shorter, or did he perhaps use something that lay yet further back? Werner Foerster,[13] for example, finds it impossible to believe that the Apocryphon in its shorter version presents an original form of a Gnostic system, or could have served as the basis for Irenaeus' account: it presents only part of the underlying system; there are contradictions and inconsistencies; and there are points at which the account in Irenaeus is clearer and more comprehensible than the Apocryphon. Similarly, Puech[14] writes that if the shorter version is the older it would be difficult to identify it with the original version of the work; but he shows some reserve with regard to the view earlier advanced by Doresse,[15] that the original document was a short treatise of non-Christian character, identical with Irenaeus' source, which later formed the basis on which our Apocryphon was constructed. Finally H. M. Schenke[16] argues that the Apocryphon is not Irenaeus' source, but a composite work the second part of which shows certain parallels with the Sophia Jesu Christi (see below). Among other things, he notes the striking fact that Irenaeus ends his extract precisely at a point where the Apocryphon shows a clear suture: thus far the exposition has taken the form of connected discourse and deals with cosmogony; from this point on it takes the form of question and answer, and the subject is soteriology. The document used by Irenaeus contained a variant form of the cosmogony presented in the Apocryphon, not that cosmogony itself.

For reasons of space it is not possible to discuss in detail the arguments advanced by these four scholars, or the divergencies between their respective views. It is however clear that Schmidt's

[13] In *Gott und die Götter*, (Festgabe E. Fascher, Berlin 1958), p. 141.
[14] op. cit., p. 330.   [15] *Vig. Chr.* 2, (1948), p. 158.
[16] *ZRGG* 14, (1962), pp. 57 ff.

opinion of the relationship between Irenaeus and the Apocryphon is no longer tenable in the form in which it was first advanced. We certainly have in both cases the same system, but whether Irenaeus' source was an earlier version of the Apocryphon itself, or another document which served as the basis for it, is still an open question. As Schenke notes,[17] comparison of other pairs of documents from Nag Hammadi, the Sophia Jesu Christi and the Epistle of Eugnostos or the Hypostasis of the Archons and the anonymous treatise in Codex II, together with the long and short recensions of the Apocryphon itself, shows that the Gnostics were in the habit of adapting and revising their documents. We have therefore to reckon with the possibility that the Coptic versions of the Apocryphon of John stand at some remove from the document used by Irenaeus.

That the Apocryphon is composite is suggested not only by the suture detected by Schenke, with the differences in form and subject-matter between the two parts, but also by the curious fact that it begins by referring to John in the third person, switches on the first page to the *first* person, and finally reverts again at the end to the third person. This suggests that the narrative framework is a later addition to a text already complete, and prompts a search for clear and unmistakable Christian elements, such as New Testament quotations or allusions. Extensive and direct quotations are conspicuous by their absence, and even such allusions as have been detected must be considered doubtful. In Till's edition only four are noted: (a) The formula 'that which is, that which has been, and that which shall be' (22.4 f.) recalls Rev. 1.19; but as W. C. van Unnik writes in a study of this formula, 'the relation between these two texts is not inevitably so that AJ depends on Apoc. 1.19'.[18] (b) At 26.18 there is a reference to 'the fount of the water of life, the light full of purity', with which Till compares Rev. 22.1; but again the parallel is scarcely so close as to suggest dependence. (c) At 59.9 ff. it is said that the ἐπίνοια of light is unattainable, and that 'although the darkness pursued her, it could not grasp her'. Here there does appear to be an echo of John 1.5, but direct dependence on John is another matter. It would seem nearer the mark to suggest a speculation inspired by John, in

[17] ibid., p. 63 n. 20.   [18] *NTS* 9, (1963), p. 93.

H

which the light which came into the world has been re-interpreted and identified with the ἐπίνοια; but then we are plunged
into the problem of priorities. Was John the inspiration for this
speculation, or could it be independent and the similarity quite
fortuitous? Or does the Apocryphon point to some older speculation upon which John is dependent? (d) The strongest claim-
ant is probably a saying of the Revealer: 'I am the one who is
with you always' (21.19; cf. Matt. 28.20).

Grant in his *Anthology*[19] adds a few more: John 'went up to
the temple' (19.9 f.; cf. Acts 3.1); the Revealer says 'John, why
do you doubt?' (21.14 f.; cf. Matt. 28.17), and speaks of instruct-
ing him 'about the perfect Man' (22.9; cf. Eph. 4.13). The
supreme God is 'invisible, because no-one has seen him' (23.21–
24.1; cf. John 1.18). The fount of the Spirit 'flowed out of the
living water of light' (26.19 ff.; cf. John 7.38); here Grant passes
over Till's reference to Rev. 22 for the previous line, but on 'he
told it to us' (26.14) cites John 1.18. At 32.13 f., 'the invisible
Spirit appointed him as God over the All', Grant quotes Rom.
9.5; but no-one seems to have noticed the closer parallel in the
following lines: 'The true God gave him all power' (cf. Matt.
28.18). Rom. 8.22 is adduced at 53.10 ff., 'This is she who works
at the whole creature [Adam] since she labours with the creature', but here caution is necessary. This translation certainly
suggests the Romans passage, and the latter may indeed be
somewhere in the background; but examination of the parallel
versions and of the translations by Till, Giversen and Krause
suggests that in these the similarity is not so close. It may indeed
be one of those cases in which conclusions based on a particular
modern translation can be misleading without some explanatory comment.

At 61.12 ff. Ialdabaoth is said to be 'ignorant of the mystery
which originated from the decree of the holy Height'; for
'mystery' Grant refers to Eph. 5.32. A closer parallel appears at
66.8, with its reference to those who 'endure all things and
suffer all things (1 Cor. 13.7) so that they may pass through the
struggle and inherit eternal life'. Finally, at 70.11 ff. Grant
identifies a whole cluster of allusions: 'They will go to the place
where the angels of impoverishment (cf. Gal. 4.9) will with-
draw, for whom there is no portion of repentance (cf. Heb.

[19] *Gnosticism. An Anthology*, pp. 69 ff.

12.17). They will all be preserved for the day on which they will be punished. All who have blasphemed against the Holy Spirit (Matt. 12.31) will be tormented in eternal punishment' (cf. Heb. 6.4–8).

The significance of these parallels will of course be variously estimated. In a document of Christian Gnosticism they are most naturally taken as allusions to the New Testament itself, but some of them are very faint echoes indeed. Now in its present form the Apocryphon *is* a Christian Gnostic document, as the narrative framework is enough to show; but was it entirely of Christian Gnostic origin, or are these 'New Testament elements' signs of a Christianising redaction of a non-Christian text? At any rate there is a striking contrast between the comparatively spasmodic introduction of such New Testament allusions and the thorough-going re-interpretation of the Genesis creation story which forms the basis of the cosmogonical section.

A further point relates to the occurrences of the name 'Christ', which in the cosmogony is assigned to a 'spark of light' to which Barbelo gives birth and which is also called Monogenes and the First-born Son of the All. At the first appearance of this figure, and in a passage including the first occurrence of the name, it is said that the Invisible Spirit 'anointed him with his goodness, so that he became perfect, faultless, and Christ, for he anointed him with the goodness of the Invisible Spirit.' Here again there are New Testament echoes, and in addition a play on the Greek words $\chi\rho\iota\sigma\tau\acute{o}\varsigma$ and $\chi\rho\eta\sigma\tau\acute{o}\varsigma$, known also from other sources.[20] There is however some variation in the texts at this point, and the Codex II version eliminates the name Christ altogether. This makes the later statement that the next aeon, Nous, 'stood up together with Christ' very sudden and abrupt, and it would certainly appear that the Berlin text is more original here, since in it the way is prepared. Consideration must however be given to the possibility that the introduction of the name is part of a process of Christianisation. Certainly there are points (e.g. 32.20 Till) at which it seems to be added almost as an afterthought. Here then is a problem which awaits closer investigation: Can it be shown that the Apocryphon as we now have it presents a Christianisation of an

[20] Cf. Bauer, *Wörterbuch*, col. 1610; Böhlig however [*Titelloses Werk*, p. 46] translates the Apocryphon passage differently.

older text, or an older system, or do the various versions suggest a movement *away from* Christianity? What, for example, is the significance of the addition at the very end of the long recension, both in Codex II and in Codex IV, of the words 'Jesus Christ. Amen', which are missing both from the Berlin text and from Codex III?

The revelation takes the form of a continuous discourse down to p. 45 of the Berlin text, where a question by John affords the opportunity for the Revealer to correct a 'false' interpretation of Gen. 1.2. Schenke, as already noted, detected a suture here, but this is open to question, although the same view was taken also by Doresse.[21] The discourse resumes for a further thirteen pages, until it is interrupted on p. 58 by two similar questions which again provide occasion for the correcting of false interpretations. It is only at p. 64 that the form changes to a dialogue, and the questions relate to soteriology. In the space of eight pages we have seven questions, the last of which leads to another long discourse, which in the Codex II version runs into the account of 'the deeds of the Redeemer', missing from the Berlin text. Does the 'new' section begin only at p. 64, or is the whole of the material from the point where Irenaeus breaks off to be regarded as later addition, perhaps in several stages? In all ten questions John in the Berlin text addresses the Revealer as 'Christ', but in each case Till notes that Codex III (CG I in Till) has the reading 'Lord', a reading supported in nine cases by Codex II, and in several also by the fragmentary Codex IV. The variant is easily explained as due to confusion of two Coptic letters in the contracted form of the word, but which was the original?

Giversen[22] notes that in the description of the deeds of the Redeemer 'it is conspicuous that the redeemer is nowhere referred to as Christ, nor as Jesus or Saviour or Lord'. Working on the basis of the Berlin text, van Unnik[23] had already written 'the role of Jesus is clearly no more than that of mediator of the true Knowledge, which is the real saving power. Jesus has no central place in the work of redemption. The figure of Jesus could come right out of the book without changing its character in any essential respect.' He found plenty of evidence that the

[21] *Secret Books*, p. 210.   [22] *Apocryphon Johannis*, p. 270.
[23] *Newly Discovered Gnostic Writings*, pp. 76 ff.

author (or redactor?) knew his New Testament intimately, for there are references at several points. 'But they are woven into an entirely different context of thought from that in which they occur in the New Testament.' In sum, 'because of its peculiar combination of ideas drawn from sharply divergent systems of thought, this document throws a special light on the rise of Gnosticism. Everything points to its having originated outside Christianity and to the enrichment of an existing system at a later stage with Christian material.'[24] It is only when we recall the role played by Hermes as mediator of *gnosis* in the Corpus Hermeticum, and the conclusions drawn by Dodd in his study of the Hermetica,[25] that such a judgment is given its full weight.

There is, then, ground for the view that the Apocryphon of John presents a Christianisation of an older non-Christian text, or at least of a non-Christian system, but is this confirmed by comparison of the different versions? Can we arrange them in chronological order and show a progressive Christianisation, or is the movement in the opposite direction? The latter conclusion would of course entail revision of van Unnik's judgment, but investigation of this question has scarcely begun, nor can it be entered into here. It must suffice to outline some aspects of the problem.

There are cases in which one of the two shorter versions uses a Greek word, the other its Coptic equivalent; but the usage is not consistent, for sometimes it is the first which uses the Coptic word and the second the Greek. And there are cases in which there seems to be an alteration in the meaning. In the longer versions, again, some of the apparent expansion fits so well into the context that we should never have suspected anything but for its absence in the shorter versions. Which direction did the development take—expansion of the shorter versions, or abridgement of the longer?

Here already two opinions have been advanced. Giversen[26] thinks Codex II more original and holds the shorter versions to be abridgements, although he admits (a) that the latter are sometimes more reliable in terms of content, and (b) that Codex

[24] ibid., p. 79.
[25] *The Bible and the Greeks*, p. 248; cf. above, p. 83 f.
[26] *Apocryphon Johannis*, p. 277.

II also has some insertions, some of them fairly lengthy. Kasser[27] on the other hand argues that it is rare for a text to be shortened, and that examination of the material peculiar to the long recension shows it to be a development of the shorter. The Berlin text he considers nearest to the original, but he considers its parallel in Codex III comparatively late.

One passage which Giversen admits to be an interpolation occurs in the account of the creation of man—a passage (Codex II, 63.29–67.10) which identifies and names the angels responsible for the making of each part of the body, the right eye and the left, for example, or the right foot and the left—there is a separate angel for the toes of each foot, and another for the toe-nails! Now it might appear that in conceding the presence of insertions Giversen has given his case away, but we must be more subtle. It is not sufficient simply to dismiss the longer version as secondary because of this passage, or other such insertions. We have to leave such sections out of the reckoning and compare the rest, in the effort to see *why* the changes have been made. If we can find the explanation for an alteration in one direction or another, this may help to solve the problem. If there are grounds for thinking that one version has been consistently modified to bring it into conformity with a particular theory, then we also have reason for considering that version to be the later. Here obviously much remains to be done.

Two final points of interest are (a) the reference at 67.10 in Codex II, at the end of the long insertion mentioned above, to the 'book of Zoroaster', which Giversen[28] suggests may indicate not only where further information may be found but also the source upon which the Apocryphon has drawn at this point, and (b) the possible significance of the document for the development of Valentinianism. Irenaeus places the Barbelognostics among the precursors of Valentinus, and comparison with known Valentinian documents may help us to trace the growth of that system. This, as we have already seen, is a point at which the Gospel of Truth may be of significance: is it possible to trace a line of development from that Gospel to the full Valentinian system, such as to show that knowledge of Barbelognostic theory in general, and the Apocryphon of John in particular, has contributed to the process? How much of the Valentinian theory

[27] *Rev. Theol. et Phil.*, 1964, pp. 144 f.   [28] *Apocryphon Johannis*, p. 281.

remains if we remove the Barbelognostic elements? Here again are problems still awaiting investigation.

3. *The Sophia Jesu Christi.*[29] Of this document two versions are extant in Coptic, one complete in the Berlin Codex and a second, of which two leaves are missing, in the Nag Hammadi library. The latter has not yet been published, but its variant readings are noted in Dr. Till's edition of the Berlin text. Part of the interest of this document lies in the fact that it has in the Nag Hammadi library a very close parallel, the Epistle of Eugnostos, so close indeed as to raise the question of literary dependence. Now the Sophia is a book of revelation, in fact a 'gospel' of the Gnostic type, containing a conversation between Jesus and the disciples upon a mountain after the Resurrection. Much of it is in the form of answers given by Jesus in response to the questions put by his hearers. Eugnostos on the other hand is a straightforward dogmatic epistle, in the form not of a dialogue but of continuous discourse, and according to some accounts without any distinctly Christian features. The question is whether Eugnostos is a development from the Sophia, by the elimination of the dialogue and of the Christian elements; or the Sophia created out of Eugnostos by the breaking up of the discourse and the insertion of the questions. In fact, this might appear to be a test case for the relation of Gnosticism to Christianity, for on the first alternative obviously we should have evidence of a movement away from Christianity, a process of de-Christianisation; whereas on the second view we should have the Christianising of a previously non-Christian text. Unfortunately, as so often happens, the issue is not quite so simple, nor are the problems so readily solved.

Doresse in one of the earliest studies of the Nag Hammadi documents[30] argued for the dependence of the Sophia upon Eugnostos, and even at one point for the view that it was composed in Coptic on the basis of Eugnostos. In this he was followed by Werner Foerster,[31] but both wrote before the publication of the Berlin text, which at the points in question varies

---

[29] Text in Till, pp. 194 ff. See also Puech in Hennecke-Schneemelcher, i, pp. 243 ff.

[30] *Vig. Chr.* 2, (1948), pp. 150 ff. Cf. Till, op. cit., p. 305.

[31] *TLZ* 79, (1954), col. 379.

to some extent from that of Nag Hammadi. Moreover Puech[32] had shown in the interval that two pages of the *Greek* text of the Sophia are preserved in one of the Oxyrhynchus papyri (POx.1081). It is more probable that translation was from Greek into Coptic than the other way, and moreover the Oxyrhynchus fragment is dated at least half a century before the Coptic texts, so that Doresse's earlier conclusion as to the original language is incorrect; in his book he has accordingly abandoned it.[33] The facts which led him to this conclusion, however, remain to be explained, as does the precise relationship of the two Coptic versions of the Sophia. This example provides an excellent illustration of the way in which apparently sound deductions may be overtaken by events, and shown to be in fact erroneous by subsequent discovery.

Eugnostos unfortunately has not yet been published, and our information has to be dug out of the apparatus to the Berlin edition of the Sophia. A final judgment on the relation between them must therefore await publication of the text of Eugnostos, but it may be noted that so far those who have gone into the matter differ in their conclusions. Doresse, as already remarked, argued for the priority of Eugnostos, but Till in his edition says 'It seems to me much more probable that SJC was the source of Eug. and not the contrary.'[34] Puech notes that the Sophia is a little longer, and 'contains here and there passages which are peculiar to it.'[35] Like Doresse, he maintains that the Sophia is only a recasting of the epistle. It should perhaps be noted here that while some of the peculiar passages are quite short and consist of a few lines only, containing a question from a disciple and words to the effect that the Saviour answered, there are one or two which extend to two or three pages; moreover there are over two pages of text before the parallel with Eugnostos begins, and some ten pages at the end where the Sophia is again quite independent.

Perhaps the fullest discussions as yet are those of H. M. Schenke and M. Krause,[36] who again take opposite sides.

---

[32] Cf. Hennecke-Schneemelcher, i, p. 245.
[33] *Secret Books*, p. 196.   [34] op. cit., p. 54.
[35] Hennecke-Schneemelcher, i, p. 248.
[36] Schenke, *ZRGG* 14, (1962), pp. 264 ff.; Krause in *Mullus*, Jahrb. f. Antike u. Christentum, Ergänzungsband i, (Münster 1964), pp. 215 ff.

Schenke states and refutes the arguments advanced by Doresse, and notes as the decisive argument in his opinion the fact that Eugnostos also contains peculiar material, one section of which lists six pairs of aeons originating from the Saviour and Pistis Sophia. These, he argues, considerably increase and complicate the number of the heavenly beings present in the Sophia, and can be recognised from their names to be the product of secondary elaboration of the original system. Moreover Eugnostos, to judge by Doresse's account of its contents, gives the impression of being put together from fragments detached from their original setting, and indeed there are points at which one can still detect the breaks. A further argument advanced by Schenke is directly countered by Krause. Schenke wrote that it is scarcely credible that any-one, even a Gnostic, should have forced a systematically ordered whole into a scheme of question and answer which destroys the run of thought. The subsequent systematisation of what was formerly unsystematic is on the other hand perfectly comprehensible. Krause affirms that this argument is not valid for the Gnostic texts, since experience repeatedly shows how clear systems through the incorporation of further ideas become ever more complicated and obscure. He cites the Apocryphon of John by way of example, and the Pistis Sophia as generally recognised to be the final product of such a process.

Previous scholars, as Schenke had already noted,[37] were not in possession of all the evidence. Doresse did not know the Berlin text of the Sophia or the Greek fragment, and while he knew the version of Eugnostos in Codex III he did not have access to the second version in Codex V. Schenke knew both the Greek fragment and the Berlin text of the Sophia, but the Nag Hammadi version was available to him only through Till's apparatus and Eugnostos only in so far as it was parallel to the Sophia or from Doresse's account of its contents. Krause's case is strengthened by the fact that it is based on the whole of the material.

His method is to examine the material peculiar to each of the documents and compare it with the material common to both. 'The document whose special material agrees in content with the text common to both is probably the primary document,

[37] op. cit., p. 265; cf. Krause, p. 217 n. 27.

the one whose special material obviously does not fit the common text is probably the secondary.'[38] Now the special material in the Sophia is more extensive than that of Eugnostos, and it does not agree with the common material. When we compare the questions of the disciples (special material) with the answers given by the Saviour (common material), we find that so far as they are not cast in general terms the questions do not fit the answers. Again, the special material breaks up sections which belong together, and there are points at which the special material does not agree with statements contained in the common matter. On the other hand the special material in Eugnostos does fit the common material. Finally, there are points at which the Sophia is confusing, because the introduction of the special material has interrupted the train of thought. When this special material is removed, we obtain an intelligible text which is close to that of Eugnostos. Eugnostos therefore is the older and the Sophia the secondary document.

Final judgment must of course await the detailed checking which can only be done when the text of Eugnostos becomes available. There is however a further point to be considered. According to Krause[39] the special material in Eugnostos, like the material common to both documents, contains no Christian ideas. Schenke[40] on the other hand affirms that Christian motifs are firmly rooted in the teaching of Eugnostos. On this point Till's edition provides an adequate basis for preliminary discussion.

In the first place it has to be noted that, apart from the common formula 'He who has ears to hear, let him hear!' (Matt. 11.15 par.), the clearest New Testament allusions in Till's brief list occur on p. 79 of the Berlin Codex, that is, in the preamble to the Sophia. Here there is a clear reference to the Transfiguration, which is however located on the Mount of Olives—in Galilee! Again, when the risen Jesus comes in his glory to the disciples, he greets them with the words 'Peace be with you! The peace which is mine I give you' (cf. Lk. 24.36; John 20.19,21,26; 14.27). The Matthean formula mentioned above occurs at four points (89.4 f., 90.13–14, 107.18–108.1 Till; the reference to 98.10–12 in Till's index is a mistake for 100.10–12), but on closer inspection every one of them proves to

[38] op. cit., p. 218.   [39] ibid.   [40] op. cit., p. 265.

be in material peculiar to the Sophia. The same holds also for
the three other citations listed by Till: 'To you it is given to
know, and to those who are worthy to know' (82.9–10; cf.
Matt. 13.11); a reference to 'those who were born of the seed of
the unclean impulse' (82.14; cf. John 1.13); and a further
reference to those who were sent 'like a drop from the light into
the world' (103.10–14; cf. John 1.9). The Christian element
in the Sophia is therefore to this extent stronger than is the
case in Eugnostos; but was Eugnostos itself completely non-
Christian?

Dr. Krause very kindly placed his synopsis of the texts of
Eugnostos at my disposal for a few days, and the following
points are drawn from his transcription. Most of them can be
readily verified from Till's edition. Codex III (77.20 ff., cf.
SJC 95.17 ff. Till) refers to the creation of 'gods and archangels
and angels for service' (cf. also 81.3, SJC 100.1). This recalls
Heb. 1.14, although the Greek loan-word in the Coptic texts is
not the one used in Hebrews. On the following page (96.10 f.
Till) the titles 'God of gods' and 'King of kings' may reflect
knowledge of Rev. 17.14, 19.16, but here of course the Old
Testament also has to be taken into account (cf. Deut. 10.17,
Dan. 2.47); nor can it be assumed that even the Old Testament
is necessarily the source of these titles. Codex III (81.5–6; not in
Till) refers to 'the church of the saints of light', and the word
ἐκκλησία recurs later in the material common to both documents (Codex III 86.16,22 and p. 82; SJC 110.11 and p. 111).
It is doubtful how much weight should be placed on such
words as ἀσπάζεσθαι, ἀσπασμός and πίστις, but ἀγάπη occurs
not only three times in the special material of the Sophia
(88.3, 99.14, 124.3), but also once in material peculiar
to Eugnostos (Codex III 82.24). Finally, there is a reference to
'the kingdom of the Son of man' (Codex III 81.13; SJC 101.6 f.),
and the title 'Son of man' appears later in conjunction with the
other title 'Saviour' (Codex III 81.21 ff.; SJC 102.15 ff.). The
phrase 'from the foundation of the world' (SJC 80.7 f., 83.11;
common material) is common in the New Testament, and there
is a passage in Codex V of Eugnostos (8.11) which with its
reference to a 'form' and a 'name' may recall Phil. 2; but again
too much should not perhaps be built on the latter point. There
is a similar passage in the special material of the Sophia (97.17–

98.4) which will require to be compared when Codex V eventually becomes available.

Once again, the significance of these resemblances will be variously estimated. At the very least, however, they seem to demand a due measure of caution over against assertions that Eugnostos is entirely non-Christian or shows no sign of Christian influence. There is nonetheless a further possibility: is the Epistle of Eugnostos itself a Christianised version of an earlier document? Here a further suggestion by Krause[41] calls for examination. He suggests that the original basis was a cosmogonical text, intended to refute three different philosophical theories regarding the origin of the world and to present in their stead a system which began with a description of the true and unbegotten God and extended down through three successive emanations to the manifestation of Chaos. This system contained some Jewish but no Christian elements, and no soteriology. The document was transformed by Eugnostos into an epistle through the addition of the appropriate framework, and one of the versions of this epistle was subsequently worked over and given the Christian framework which we now find in the Sophia.

Such a process is not in itself improbable, although confirmation of the theory must await the publication of all the texts. The very existence of differing versions of certain documents in the Nag Hammadi library shows that such redactional activity did take place, but on the other hand there must always be an element of speculation in the reconstruction of hypothetical 'basic documents' from existing texts when we have no originals to work on. Two points however may be significant: (a) if Krause is correct, and Eugnostos or its *Grundschrift* contained Jewish but no Christian elements, we should have a further pointer to some connection between Judaism and Gnostic origins; and (b) if the *Grundschrift* was of a philosophical character we may have to revise some of our ideas as to the development of Gnosticism. Was it from mythology to philosophy, or did systems originally philosophical degenerate into myth and finally into fantasy? Or should we think of a development from mythology to philosophical mysticism, followed by a degeneration? Conclusions on this point would obviously have a bearing

[41] op. cit., p. 222.

on the place of particular documents in the whole process of development.

Two further points may be noted in conclusion: (a) if Eugnostos or its *Grundschrift* is non-Christian, this does not necessarily mean that it is *pre*-Christian, at least in the sense that it dates back before the Christian era. It is entirely possible for Gnosticism in some of its forms to have developed parallel to but independently of Christianity, in approximately the same period, and for some of its documents to have been subsequently Christianised by the more specifically Christian Gnostics. (b) As Schenke observes,[42] we have to reckon in the history of Gnosticism not only with Christianisation but also with de-Christianisation. It is probably a mistake to envisage the development as moving always and consistently in the one direction, and the same may be true also of the relation between Gnosticism and philosophy. Here again a great deal needs to be done in the way of detailed investigation before we can attempt to formulate general conclusions.

4. *De Resurrectione* (*The Epistle to Rheginus*).[43] The double title in this case calls for explanation: De Resurrectione is the Latin form of the title 'the Treatise concerning the Resurrection' which appears in the manuscript at the end of the text. The final leaf containing the title was not however among the leaves of this Codex which were brought to Zürich, but was subsequently discovered among the Cairo fragments published by Labib.[44] Working on the Zürich portion only, Puech and Quispel in their pioneer study took the document to be a letter to Rheginus, otherwise unknown, who is addressed in the opening lines and at two other points in the text. The discovery and identification of the missing leaf later revealed the real title, which was accordingly adopted for the edition of the text; but the other title had already to some extent become established.

This document is the third of those contained in the Jung Codex, and follows immediately on the Gospel of Truth.

[42] op. cit., p. 266.
[43] Text with French, German and English translations in Malinine, Puech, Quispel and Till, *De Resurrectione*, (Zürich and Stuttgart 1963). Cf. Puech-Quispel, *Vig. Chr.* 8, (1954), pp. 40 ff.
[44] *Coptic Gnostic Papyri*, plates 1 and 2.

Comparatively short, it extends to seven pages only and belongs unmistakably to the documents of Christian Gnosticism, or more particularly the Valentinian school. As yet it has not attracted a great deal of attention, and apart from the pioneer article mentioned above and the material assembled in the edition only a few articles have been devoted to it. J. Zandee[45] has compared its teaching with that of the Gospel of Philip, and noted some striking similarities which serve to confirm its general Valentinian character. W. C. van Unnik[46] made it the subject of two lectures, and C. F. D. Moule[47] has drawn upon it in a study of Paul's teaching.

The first point to be observed is the difference, indeed the contrast, between this document and such works as the Apocryphon of John, the Sophia Jesu Christi, or the Epistle of Eugnostos. As we have seen, there is some possibility that the three latter works may go back to older documents, or to an older system, which has in them been Christianised. The De Resurrectione however has not as yet prompted any such intriguing speculations. On the contrary, the author clearly takes his stand within the Church. As van Unnik notes, 'He quotes the Gospel and St. Paul; his ideas have parallels in non-Gnostic authors and are based solely on the work of Jesus Christ.' Indeed the centrality of Jesus is a notable feature of the document, and this not only as a Teacher or as the Revealer of Gnosis: the resurrection of believers is firmly based upon what has happened in Christ. The resurrection is not an illusion but the truth, a reality, and 'came into being through our Lord the Saviour Jesus Christ' (48.10–19). The Son of God was also Son of Man, in order that as Son of God he might vanquish death and that 'through the Son of Man the restoration into the Pleroma might take place' (44.21–33).

As these last words show, it is a Gnostic document; 'restoration' and 'pleroma' are both technical terms in the vocabulary of Valentinianism, and there are other indications also of its Gnostic character elsewhere in the text. Yet this is a form of Gnosticism much nearer to what we know as 'orthodox' Christainity. This may serve to warn against undue readiness to formulate sweeping and comprehensive generalisations about

[45] *Nederlands Theol. Tijdschr.* 16, pp. 361 ff.
[46] *JEH* 15, (1964), 141 ff., 153 ff.   [47] *NTS* 12, (1966), pp. 106 ff.

the nature of Gnosticism. If some of the Nag Hammadi texts still unpublished present 'purely Gnostic' revelations, as Doresse[48] affirms, and others may be described as 'Gnostics disguised as Christians', there were other Gnostic thinkers who started from some point of Christian doctrine and developed it, or re-interpreted it, in a Gnostic direction.

A second feature is the emphasis placed in this text upon faith, and in particular upon faith in contrast to philosophical argument:

'If there is anyone who does not believe, it is not possible to persuade him, for it is the place of faith, and does not belong to persuasion' (46.2–7).

'We came to know the Son of Man, and we came to believe that he rose again from the dead, and this is he of whom we say that he became the destruction of death, so that it is a great one on whom they believe. Those who believe are immortal' (46.14–21). On the other hand, as the editors justly note,[49] the author 'shows a certain animosity with regard to the endless discussions to which the philosophers devoted themselves, these eternal *disputationes in utramque partem* on such subjects as the immortality of the soul' (cf. 43.25–35). For him Christianity is the absolute truth, the final answer to all the vain discussions of the philosophical schools. In this, as they observe, he is akin to Justin or the Clement of the Recognitions, a man trained in Greek philosophy, and especially in Platonism, who has yet abandoned it because it did not satisfy his deepest needs.

Not only is there this emphasis upon faith, but it is clearly the Christian faith which after his own fashion the author desires to commend. As we have seen, he speaks of 'our Lord the Saviour Jesus Christ', and describes him as both Son of God and Son of Man. There is a reference to the Transfiguration:

For if thou remember reading in the Gospel that Elias appeared and Moses with him, do not think that the resurrection is an illusion. It is no illusion, but it is the truth. Nay rather it is fitting for us to say that the world is an illusion rather than the resurrection.

(48.6–16)

Finally there is a reference to 'the Apostle', who is clearly Paul,

[48] *Secret Books*, p. 146.   [49] *De Resurrectione*, p. xviii.

for it is followed by a catena of quotations from the Pauline epistles (45.23–9).

Other New Testament echoes and allusions can be detected at various points, but this Christian material is built up into something quite different. In particular, as Puech and Quispel noted in their pioneer study,[50] the Pauline mysticism has been interpreted in terms of solar theology:

> As the Apostle said, we suffered with him, and we arose with him, and we went to heaven with him. But if we are made manifest in this world wearing him, we are his beams and we are encompassed by him until our setting, which is our death in this life. We are drawn upward by him like the beams by the sun, without being held back by anything. This is the spiritual resurrection which swallows up the psychic alike with the fleshly.
>
> (45.24–46.2)

Here we touch upon one of the most interesting and intriguing, yet sometimes also frustrating, aspects of the study of these new texts: the detailed tracing out of the connections, the influences which were at work, the way in which these writers thought, the reasons which led them to a particular interpretation, or re-interpretation, of the passages before them. The question here is not whether they were right or wrong, 'orthodox' or 'heretical', but how and why they came to their conclusions. In most cases there is a certain logic about their procedure, even if by 'orthodox' standards it is a perverse logic. Given a particular interpretation of a passage from Paul, its association with particular interpretations of other passages, and in some cases a link with some philosophical or other motif in the contemporary world, and the whole theory begins to fall into place. In other words, intensive study of these texts may help to show not only what the Gnostics thought but why and how they developed their theories. Here however we are still only at the beginning of our investigations.

A further point relates to the 'solar theology' mentioned above. There is no question that the first beginnings of this kind of thinking go far back before the Christian period. Wendland[51]

---

[50] *Vig. Chr.* 8, (1954), pp. 43 f.; cf. *De Resurrectione*, p. xiv.
[51] *Die hellenistisch-römische Kultur*, (Tübingen 1912), p. 158.

for example long ago wrote that the Chaldean solar and astral theology, already combined in the second century B.C. with advanced astronomical knowledge and with the Stoic philosophy, was united in Posidonius with the stream of Greek mysticism and the conception of the substantial unity of the soul with the realm of the stars. It was however only in the second Christian century and later that this solar theology reached the peak of its influence. The references adduced by the editors of our document[52] are significant: Plutarch, Philostratus, Proclus, the emperor Julian. And this is the very period which saw the rise of Gnosticism proper. It may be that such passages as Eph. 5.14 show these ideas already in currency at an earlier period, but here in Ephesians we have a definitely Christian hymn, and moreover we have to allow for the probable influence of the Old Testament (cf. Is. 60.1). It is not unusual, again, for something which began as poetic metaphor to be later hardened into a prosaic statement of fact. The point is that whatever the ultimate origins, and whatever the anticipations and adumbrations which we may detect, it was the second century which saw the real explosion, in Gnosticism, in Mithraism and other solar religions, in certain aspects of contemporary philosophy. We must of course endeavour to trace the whole chain of connection back to the ultimate origins, but it is dangerous in the extreme to assume that the entire content of later speculation was already present at earlier stages. We have also to try to understand the 'explosion' in the context and setting of its own period. Why was this kind of thinking so widely prevalent at this particular time?

It would be too much to say that the De Resurrectione is a masterly study; indeed at first sight it appears rather a rambling discourse. Certainly it falls far short of the massive and comprehensive treatment of Tertullian's treatise on the subject, and the author seems to stand on a rather different intellectual level from a Paul or a John, or from the best of the early Fathers. This may however be due in part to the difficulties of the subject, which the author expressly mentions (44.39–45.2), and in part to the fact that it is a comparatively early attempt to deal with these problems. The editors have provided a clue to the structure which shows that the work is in fact composed to a deliberate pattern: after a general introduction (43.25–44.3),

[52] *De Resurrectione*, pp. xiv–xv.

I

the theme is stated (44.3–12) and the main argument follows (44.12–47.1), rounded off by a brief summary (47.1–4); the following section deals with objections (47.4–49.9), and then comes a paraenetic conclusion (49.9–36), the document ending with an epilogue and greetings (49.37–50.16).

In the argument there are some remarkable contrasts with what is usually considered the 'Gnostic' attitude; for example, there is apparently no rejection of the resurrection of the flesh:

> For if thou wert not in the flesh, thou didst take on flesh when thou didst come into this world. Wherefore shouldst thou not take on the flesh when thou goest up into the aeon? That which is better than the flesh is for it the cause of life.
>
> (47.4–10)

This however appears to be contradicted later (the passage unfortunately is damaged):

> ... the members which are visible (but) dead will not be saved, for it is only the living (members?) that are within them which were to rise again. What then is the resurrection? It is the revelation at every moment of those who have arisen.
>
> (47.38–48.6)

Here we have to keep in mind the various theories which were current about the resurrection in the second century.[53] It was not simply a question of acceptance of the doctrine, or of its rejection in favour of belief in the immortality of the soul alone. It was a question also of the interpretation placed upon the doctrine, what it was held to signify; for there were those who affirmed that 'death' meant ignorance of God, and that in coming to knowledge of the truth, in accepting the Gospel, the believer was raised from death to walk in newness of life. Or it could be held that resurrection was deliverance from the tomb of the body, or again that it involved a transformation of the physical body into a spiritual one. It is not difficult to see how at one point or another an appeal could be made to Paul's teaching, but the combination of different elements of Pauline thought into a new synthesis, and the association of such

[53] Cf. *Vig. Chr.* 8, (1954), pp. 40 ff.; *De Resurrectione*, pp. x ff.; *JEH* 15, (1964), pp. 153 ff.

elements with other ideas from very different sources, might well lead to conclusions which Paul himself would not have countenanced.

The interest of the De Resurrectione lies (a) in its presentation of the doctrine—not perhaps an epoch-making treatment, yet one that is instructive as showing the thought of the period; (b) in its presentation of a Gnostic discussion of a theme which attracted the attention of other writers also—Justin, Athenagoras, Theophilus, Tertullian. As van Unnik notes,[54] the doctrine does not appear on the whole to have been a centre of debate in the first century, while it was already a fixed element in the Creed by the third; but in the second century it was a highly controversial subject. Finally the document is of interest (c) for the persistence and utilisation of Pauline themes and echoes. It enables us to see how a thinker of the second century could understand and interpret Paul from the point of view of his own later tradition.

That it is a Valentinian document has been sufficiently shown by Puech and Quispel.[55] It makes use of technical terms from the Valentinian vocabulary, and quotes a passage from Colossians with a variant characteristic of that school; and in addition to the Valentinian elements in point of content there are also the similarities to the Gospel of Philip, to which Zandee has drawn attention.[56] Whether we can identify the author more precisely is however another question. Puech and Quispel would date it after the Gospel of Truth, and suggest that the author was either a leader of the 'oriental' school of Valentinianism or Valentinus himself; and they incline to favour the latter alternative.[57] For van Unnik, on the other hand, this remains uncertain.[58] It is not impossible that the same man wrote both the De Resurrectione and the Gospel of Truth, and other works too for that matter, but the fact remains that we have no really adequate basis for a decision; and overhasty identifications tend to be overtaken by later events. It

[54] *JEH* 15, (1964), p. 156.
[55] *Vig. Chr.* 8, (1954), pp. 46 ff.; *De Resurrectione*, pp. xx ff.
[56] *Ned. Theol. Tijdschr.* 16, pp. 361 ff.
[57] *Vig. Chr.* 8, (1954), p. 50; *De Resurrectione*, p. xxxiii.
[58] *JEH* 15, (1964), p. 144. Cf. Haenchen, *ThR* 30, (1964), p. 57 on the difficulty of assigning both this work and the Gospel of Truth to Valentinus.

would seem therefore advisable to describe the De Resurrectione simply as a work of the Valentinian school, although the possibility does exist that it may go back to Valentinus himself. In the present state of our knowledge we can say no more on this point.

5. *The Hypostasis of the Archons and the Anonymous Treatise from Codex II.* These two documents may be taken together, since there is a certain connection between them. Passages from the one can be adduced to shed light upon the other, although it should at once be added that there are also considerable differences. A further question, which has yet to be examined in detail, is the relation between these documents, or the system which they presuppose, and the system presented in such works as the Apocryphon of John, the Sophia Jesu Christi and Eugnostos.

The Hypostasis and the anonymous treatise were first made available in the photographic edition published by Labib, and were translated into German by H. M. Schenke.[59] In the case of the anonymous treatise, Schenke thought that he had almost the whole document in the fourteen pages accessible to him. It would then have been slightly longer than the immediately preceding Hypostasis. The full text however has now been published by Böhlig and Labib,[60] and a further seventeen pages have been added. As the Nag Hammadi library amply shows, it is dangerous to attempt a calculation of the probable length of a fragmentary Gnostic text unless there is some kind of external evidence upon which to work; we cannot tell what modifications, expansions or elaborations may have taken place, and the fact that, for example, a particular episode or motif occurs near the end in one document does not mean that it was also near the end in another. It should be added that Schenke was prompt to publish a correction when he learned the facts.[61]

[59] Labib, *Coptic Gnostic Papyri*, plates 134 ff., 145 ff.; Schenke, *TLZ* 1958, cols. 661 ff. [Hypostasis]; 1959, 243 ff.

[60] *Die koptisch-gnostische Schrift ohne Titel aus Codex II von Nag Hammadi*, (Berlin 1962).

[61] Leipoldt-Schenke, *Koptisch-gnostische Schriften aus den Papyrus-Codices von Nag-Hammadi*, (Hamburg-Bergstedt 1960), p. 84. This volume includes the Hypostasis, but not the anonymous treatise. An edition of the Hypostasis by R. A. Bullard is in preparation.

Between them these texts extend to some forty pages, so that space does not admit of detailed discussion here. The Hypostasis, after an introductory sentence which might almost be a title, begins with a quotation of Eph. 6.12, ascribed to 'the great Apostle Paul', and professes to be a reply to a question about the powers. There appear to be no obvious Christian elements until near the end, where we find a reference to 'the Spirit of truth whom the Father has sent' (144.35; cf. John 14.26), and to 'the unction of life eternal' (145.2). On the other hand the document is clearly a re-interpretation of Genesis of the Barbelo-gnostic type. It begins with the boast of Jaldabaoth, quoting Is. 46.9, and continues roughly parallel with the Apocryphon of John, but in summary form and with variations of detail, through the narrative of the creation of man to the birth of Cain and Abel, here the children of Adam and Eve. The statement that God looked upon the gifts of Abel, and later spoke to Cain, may be due to a failure to revise this section in a Gnostic sense; or it might possibly reflect a closer proximity to the original Genesis story. The narrative continues to the story of the Flood, where it introduces the figure of Norea, here apparently the wife of Noah (elsewhere she is the wife of Seth or Shem[62]). At this point questions arise as to the relation of our document to a 'Book of Norea' mentioned by Epiphanius (Pan. 26.1,3–9), which has the same story but with some variations. Refused admission to the ark, Norea destroys it, according to Epiphanius three times over. Menaced by the archons, she appeals for help, and an angel comes down from heaven—and proceeds to reveal to her the story of the origin of things as it had already been recorded above. Near the end the Hypostasis reports the fettering of Jaldabaoth and his imprisonment in Tartarus, and the repentance of his son Sabaoth, who is set over the seventh heaven and called 'god of the powers'. Following the reference mentioned above to 'the unction of life eternal', the document closes: 'Then they will cast away from them blind thought, and trample down the death of the powers (cf. SJC 125.19–126.11), and go up to the infinite light where this seed is. Then the powers will leave their seasons, and their angels weep over their destruction, and their demons over their death. Then all the sons of light (cf. Qumran!) shall know the truth, their true root,

[62] Cf. Leipoldt-Schenke, p. 70; Böhlig, op. cit., pp. 31 f.

the Father of the All and the Holy Spirit. They will all say with one voice: Righteous is the truth of the Father, and the Son is over all and through all for ever and ever. Holy, holy, holy. Amen.' (pl. 145 Labib).

There is evidently a slight Christian element in this document, but it is only slight, which once again raises the question of the possible Christianisation of older material. Again, why the repentance and rehabilitation of Sabaoth? What is the relation of this motif to the Hippolytan account of the theory of Basilides, where the Great Archon has a son much wiser than himself, who sits beside him, upon whom the light of the Gospel descends, and who is subsequently identified as Christ? According to Epiphanius, again, Noah put his trust in the archon, the god of this world, whereas Norea revealed the higher powers; but in the Hypostasis, in Schenke's view, Noah relies upon the righteous God who stands between the evil Demiurge and the realm of light, and this is one of Schenke's reasons for rejecting the identification of the Hypostasis with the Book of Norea. In the latter view he may be correct, but *is* the Hypostasis at variance with Epiphanius? Or has Schenke himself been misled through the identifying the ἄρχων of the powers (140.8) as Sabaoth, who is *later* given the title 'god of the powers' (143.23)? If the archon is Jaldabaoth, the two texts are in complete harmony on this point.

The anonymous work has been described by some writers as an apocalypse, but Böhlig takes a different view. He claims that the document is a polemical tract directed against the theory found in Hesiod's Theogony: that Chaos lay at the origin of all things. 'The gods of this world,' it begins, 'and men too, all say that nothing existed before Chaos, but I will demonstrate that they are all in error.' Chaos, to summarise, is darkness, a shadow—and a shadow pre-supposes something to cast the shadow. But if Chaos is thus secondary, what is the primal beginning? As Böhlig says,[63] 'the author does not have an easy task in answering this question. In the closely related Hypostasis of the Archons all this is much more clearly handled.'

Briefly, through the action of Pistis Sophia a veil is interposed between the higher and lower regions, and Chaos is the shadow created by this veil. Pistis Sophia is disturbed at the conse-

[63] *Wiss. Zeitschr. Halle* 10, (1961), pp. 1065 f.

quences of her action, and creates an archon from Chaos to set it in order. This is Jaldabaoth, and the document continues with the exposition of a system like that of the Apocryphon of John. Here however it is not a simple and straightforward exposition, for the course of the narrative is interrupted again and again by the introduction of mythological motifs. Böhlig justly speaks of *Kompilationsfreudigkeit*, and expresses the opinion that we are here at a later stage of the mythology. There is at one point a shaking of the heavens, which seems to reflect the myth of the Titans; later the legend of Cupid and Psyche is drawn upon, and later still there are references to the legend of the phoenix, to the crocodile, and to 'the bulls of Egypt' which have as a mystery the sun and moon. At several places Böhlig notes the possibility of an interpolation, notably in the transference of the repentance of Sabaoth to an earlier point in the system. The general impression left is that an originally simple system has been elaborated and expanded by the incorporation of additional material, which has not always been successfully assimilated into the context. Sometimes indeed the result is quite incongruous: one wonders how the seven virgins (153.32 ff.) contrived to handle thirty zithers, with harps and trumpets in addition! But Böhlig plausibly suggests that the virgins represent the planets (and the days of the week) and the instruments the days of the month.

As already noted, Böhlig rejects the view that this document is an apocalypse, and argues that it is a polemical tract. On this I am happy to agree, the more especially since I shall have cause to differ at a later point. It certainly begins as a polemical tract, but it develops into something more: a cosmogony running into a description of the final *apocatastasis*; and there are certainly elements of an 'apocalyptic' character in the description of the last things, the coming of the new aeon and the annihilation of evil.

Christian elements are present, but they are by no means prominent.[64] Jesus is mentioned twice only, and in a subordinate role. On the other hand Böhlig remarks 'That the Christian influences in the Gnostic thought of our text at least are greater than they might sometimes appear is shown by the introduction of New Testament words at important points.' There are quotations of New Testament passages, but they are re-interpreted

[64] Böhlig-Labib, p. 33.

and even on occasion textually modified. In many cases the Christian form is present, but that is all: 'for our Gnostics the Christian form was a form without content; for it was empty when Jesus Christ no longer formed its centre.' Lest these last words be thought too great a concession to the view which would see Gnosticism as entirely a movement away from Christianity, it should be added that Böhlig suggests that one of the references to Jesus (153.26) may be a secondary addition. The process in fact was not a simple one, for we have evidence in other texts both for Christianisation and for de-Christianisation.

The significance of these two documents lies first in the fact that they present affinities with other documents, as well as differences from them, and thus show how the Gnostics could adapt and modify their teachings to meet particular situations. Here there is need for a detailed comparison of these texts with one another, and with such other documents as the Apocryphon of John, to determine their mutual relationships and relative dates. In the process we may find much to learn about the development of Gnostic theory. Secondly, there are a number of points at which they may shed light on ideas contained in texts outside this immediate group. For example, the Hypostasis (140.1–3) uses the words 'the virgin whom the powers did not defile', and the same phrase is used in the Gospel of Philip (103.31 Labib). Here we have Gnostic use of an older motif, going back to Jewish legend. Now the Hypostasis provides an explanation earlier (137.20 ff.) in the story of the archons' abortive attempt upon Adam's 'spiritual' wife, although the phrase itself refers neither to this spiritual wife nor to Eve, but to Eve's daughter. Are we then at liberty to use the Hypostasis to explain Philip? Or have we a motif which has come to them along different lines of tradition? Is it possible to trace these developments? Again, Philip speaks of a veil or curtain (132.21 ff.), and both the Hypostasis (142.5 ff.) and the anonymous work set at the beginning of the whole cosmic (and supra-cosmic) process an act of Pistis Sophia which results in the coming into being of a veil between the higher and the lower regions. Perhaps we may also link with these the rather obscure passage at the beginning of the Gospel of Truth (17.9 ff.) concerning the operations of Error. A further example is a passage in the anonymous work about the trees in paradise (158.6 ff.), at which Böhlig compares log. 19 of the Gospel of Thomas. In each of these cases we have the same or a similar motif utilised in different documents. It would obviously be a mistake to assume without further ado that one document explains another, especially when the former is the later of the two; but comparison and analysis may provide valuable insights into the use of such motifs, the ways in which they were adapted and re-interpreted. At present we are still scarcely beyond the stage of noting the similarities and collecting the material.

Thirdly, Böhlig at a number of points draws attention to Manichean parallels, and remarks that we may see in the myths of our texts preliminary forms which furnished the materials for Mani. Here again we have evidence for developments within the Gnostic movement, in the ways in which the Manicheans took over, and sometimes adapted to their own ideas, materials already in use among the older sects. Fourth, both the Hypostasis and the anonymous treatise refer to other documents, the Book of Norea, the Book of Solomon, the Sacred Book, and so on, which may with some justice be assumed to be among their sources—and some of these may yet prove to be included among the other documents in the Nag Hammadi collection. This however remains to be seen. It is dangerous to assume from similarity of title that we have the actual book—we have as it is three different Apocalypses associated with the name of James in the Nag Hammadi library alone, two works associated with Thomas, distinct from the Infancy Gospel previously known, and a Gospel of Philip which has nothing to do with the one mentioned by Epiphanius. Also the Gospel of the Egyptians from Nag Hammadi appears to have no connection with the document of the same title quoted by Clement of Alexandria. Finally, there is the fact that while the Christian element in these documents is often slight and sometimes appears to be secondary, the Jewish is integral to the whole structure, for these works are in large measure re-interpretations of Old Testament material. Indeed there are points (e.g. the anonymous work 161.21 ff.) at which the whole speculation seems to be built upon a play on Hebrew or Aramaic words. This confirms, were confirmation needed, the significance of the Jewish contribution to the development of Gnosticism, although as already noted in an earlier chapter the fact that the material is Jewish does not necessarily mean that the people who moulded it into these systems were themselves Jews. We have also to take account of the introduction in the anonymous treatise and elsewhere of motifs derived from Greek mythology; a passage in the Gospel of Truth (29.11–14) appears to be inspired by the Iliad of Homer; and there are various reactions to and attitudes towards philosophy. These texts in short provide some insight into a period of considerable intellectual ferment, in which an emergent Christianity was striving to find a foothold and maintain itself, and experiments in syncretism of one kind or another were a common feature.

6.   *Gnostic Apocalypses: The Apocalypse of Adam.* As already noted, Böhlig rejects the view that the anonymous treatise in Codex II is an apocalypse. An apocalypse, he says, 'is a revelation, whose actual or fictitious recipient is normally named.' This literary form was frequently employed in late Judaism and in early Christianity, and the vision which belongs to the very nature of this category makes the use of myth readily comprehensible. But the mythical content of a work does not necessarily make it an apocalypse. Böhlig's point is certainly valid, but as we have seen there are elements of an 'apocalyptic' character in the work, in the section dealing with the End, the coming of the new aeon, and the final *apocatastasis*. Some consideration of the nature of 'apocalypse' would therefore seem to be called for at the outset.

A convenient starting-point is provided by the comprehensive introduction to the section 'Apocalypses and Related Subjects' in the Hennecke-Schneemelcher *NT Apocrypha*.[65] Here a distinction is made between different types of apocalypse within the Jewish tradition, those for example which report a vision and on the other hand those which profess to relate a farewell discourse by Enoch, Moses, or some other such figure from the past. The Jewish apocalypses contain revelations not only about the last things but also on the Beyond, on heaven and hell, and so on; their main interest however is not in problems of cosmology or theodicy but in eschatology. Among the characteristic features noted are the doctrine of the two ages, the 'apocalyptic

[65] Hennecke-Schneemelcher, ii, (ET: London 1965), pp. 581 ff.

pessimism' with its extreme devaluation of this present age, and the corresponding intensification of hope for and speculation about the age to come. Another feature is the use of surveys of history in the form of prophecy, which frequently give a clue to the date of these works: 'the point at which the history loses precision and accuracy is the moment of writing'.[66]

Early Christianity to a large extent shared the thought-world and temper of Jewish Apocalyptic, and took over much of the older Jewish material, whether in the form of concepts or imagery or in that of actual documents, which were Christianised by more or less extensive editing. The Church also produced its own Christian apocalypses, some of which were to exercise a considerable influence upon the literature and art of later centuries. There is however a shift of emphasis, through the concern of Christian apocalyptic with the Parousia and later with anti-Christ and the after-life. The latter, says Vielhauer,[67] while in the New Testament subsidiary to the Parousia expectation, 'are the two main themes around which Christian Apocalyptic revolves from the middle of the second century.'

The Gnostic apocalypses with which we are here concerned were not yet available to Vielhauer, and he could do no more than refer to the survey provided by Doresse.[68] He did however note two points: (a) that the contents of the works entitled 'Apocalypse' appear to be 'extensively cosmological and soteriological, and not of an eschatological-apocalyptic nature'; and (b) that on the other hand apocalyptic material is to be found in documents which carry other labels. 'The designations of form which these writings often carry in their titles should not be understood in the traditional sense as literary characterisations.'[69]

The 'apocalyptic pessimism' with its devaluation of this present age provides of course an obvious affinity with Gnosticism, and is indeed a part of the evidence to which appeal is made in support of the theory of a pre-Christian Jewish Gnosticism. Gnosticism and Apocalyptic are not however identical; difficult as it may be to distinguish them, the effort must nevertheless be made, and one criterion is already available in the

---

[66] Quoted from C. K. Barrett, *The NT Background*, (London 1956), p. 231.
[67] op. cit., p. 600.
[68] op. cit., p. 599, referring to Doresse, *Secret Books*, pp. 146–248.
[69] ibid.

first point noted above from Vielhauer. Jewish apocalyptic has beyond question contributed to the development of Gnosticism, but here again there has been a transposition of older material into a different key.

Of the apocalypses which immediately concern us, three may be briefly dealt with. As Böhlig notes, the Apocalypse of Paul and the two Apocalypses of James form a fairly homogeneous group, linked with two leading figures of the early Church. The Apocalypse of Adam, he thinks, was associated with them only because it belongs to the same literary type, for here he finds Jewish and Hellenistic Gnosis indeed, but not Christian.[70] A third Apocryphon of James in the Jung Codex has no connection with the two in Codex V.[71]

The brief *Apocalypse of Paul* is an account of Paul's ascent into the heavens, evidently inspired by 2 Cor. 12.2. It begins on the way to Jericho, and indeed as later appears 'on the mountain of Jericho' (19.11 ff.), which is of course a purely artificial setting; a mountain is the conventional place for a revelation. The actual ascent begins at the third heaven, and passes at once to the fourth, where a soul is under examination. Condemned at the mouth of three witnesses (cf. Deut. 19.15), it is cast down into a body. Entering the fifth and sixth heavens, Paul sees his 'fellow-apostles' going with him. In the seventh he meets an old man, with whom he has a long discussion, and who only allows him to go further on presentation of a sign. The further ascent up to the tenth heaven is merely related, with but little in the way of description.

This apocalypse is not the one known to Dante,[72] although there are links: in the fourth heaven Paul is told to look down on the earth (19.25 ff.; cf. Apoc. Pauli 13); that Apocalypse also introduces an old man (Apoc. Pauli 20), there identified as Enoch. This however would not fit our apocalypse, where the old man appears to be a 'guardian'; Böhlig suggests Sabaoth. Finally there are the judgment scenes, but these in the

---

[70] Böhlig-Labib, *Apokalypsen*, p. 11.

[71] Cf. Puech in Hennecke-Schneemelcher, i, pp. 333 ff.; van Unnik, *Newly Discovered Gnostic Documents*, pp. 80 ff.; Zandee, *Ned. Theol. Tijdschr.* 17, (1963), pp. 401 ff. An edition of this document is in preparation.

[72] Böhlig-Labib, *Apokalypsen*, p. 18; cf. Hennecke-Schneemelcher, ii, pp. 755 ff.

Apocalypse are much more fully elaborated. Any attempt to trace a connection between the two documents must be highly speculative.

The first *Apocalypse of James* is of a different type, and takes the form of a dialogue between James and Jesus, the first part of which (24.10–30.11) falls before the death of Jesus, the second (31.5–42.19) after the Resurrection. Between these sections is an account of James's sorrow at the sufferings of Jesus, of his ascent of 'the mountain called Gaugela' with his disciples, and of his ignorance that there is a Comforter (cf. John 14.16 etc.). James is given the name 'James the Just' (32.2 f.) and is addressed as 'my brother', although it is said that he is not a brother materially (24.12–15); in other words he is regarded as an adoptive brother. Jesus is regularly addressed as 'Rabbi'.

The document does not lend itself readily to presentation in summary form, and only a few points can be noted. The risen Lord says 'Never have I endured any kind of suffering, nor was I tormented. And this people did not do me any evil' (31.18–22). Rather does the responsibility rest with the archons. Here we seem to have something of a Docetic Christology, and certainly the responsibility, which in the canonical tradition tends to be transferred from the Romans to the Jews, is here transferred from the Jews to the heavenly powers who rule this world (cf. 1 Cor. 2.8). Again, suffering is prophesied for James, and at this he is sorely disturbed; but he is comforted by Jesus (32.10 ff.), who then instructs him how to reply to the questions of the 'guardians' (33.6 ff.). To this section, as Böhlig notes, corresponds a passage in Irenaeus, the Greek text of which is preserved by Epiphanius.[73] References to Sophia and Achamoth, among other details, point to Valentinianism. The text unfortunately is damaged towards the end. A point of interest here, however, is the connection of this text, and through it of the Valentinian school, with the Jewish Christianity which gave so high a place to James. A possible link with the Hypostasis of the Archons is provided by a reference to casting away 'blind thought, the fetter of the flesh which surrounds thee' (27.3–6; cf. HA 145.5 ff.). This *may* reflect a certain antipathy towards philosophy, such as we know to have been a characteristic of some groups of Gnostics, but here again care is necessary. The

[73] *Adv. haer.* i.14.4 Harvey; Epiph. *Pan.* 36.3.2–6.

apocalypse uses the Greek word διάνοια, the Hypostasis a Coptic equivalent, and this word has a wide range of meaning. If some of its meanings would favour the suggestion of an antipathy to philosophy, others could be so understood only indirectly, if at all. We have therefore first to examine what the word meant for the Gnostics, but this cannot be undertaken here.

Links with Jewish Christianity may be detected also in the *second Apocalypse of James*, which is formally a speech delivered by James in Jerusalem prior to his martyrdom (Böhlig aptly compares the case of Stephen in Acts). In the account of the martyrdom, strict attention is paid to the Jewish regulations regarding stoning, and the description recalls the tradition reported by Hegesippus.[74] There are also links with the account of the death of James in the pseudo-Clementines.[75] Such features strengthen Daniélou's case for a connection between Jewish Christianity and Gnosticism, and might seem to entail also a reconsideration of H. J. Schoeps' claim that the Ebionites of the Clementines were not Gnostic but anti-Gnostic. Here again however caution is required. It has become abundantly clear that whatever the source from which they drew their material the Gnostics made of it something new. Pseudo-Clementine parallels to a Gnostic text do not therefore make either the Clementines Gnostic or the Gnostics Jewish-Christian; they merely indicate that at some point there is a connection, whether through borrowing on one side or the other, or through re-action against the 'false' teaching of the other group, or through their common dependence on older tradition, which each may have adapted to its own ends. Here once again there is need for careful and detailed analysis and comparison. Sweeping generalisations based on superficial resemblances are out of place, and merely confuse the issue.

The content of the document has been analysed in detail by Böhlig. Formally, after the introduction, it is a speech by James delivered from the fifth step of the Temple, and includes such statements as: 'Now am I rich in *gnosis* and have a single Father' (47.7 ff.); 'I am the first son who was begotten . . . the beloved, . . . the righteous, . . . the son of the Father' (49.5 ff.). As Böhlig notes,[76] this gives James a position little inferior to

[74] Cf. Kittel, *TWB*, iv, pp. 961 ff.   [75] Böhlig-Labib, *Apokalypsen*, p. 64.
[76] ibid., p. 28 and the notes to the text.

that of Jesus himself. The speech goes on to relate an appearance of Jesus, who as in the first apocalypse greets James as 'my brother', an address immediately explained by Mary (50.11 ff.). Then follows a revelation given by Jesus expounding the Gnostic doctrine of the Father and the Demiurge, and explaining the place and function of James: 'Thy father is not my Father, but my Father is become a father to thee' (51.19 ff.); 'Thou art not the redeemer and helper of strangers; thou art a redeemer and helper of those who are mine, but now are thine' (55.15 ff.). At the close, in response to Jesus' command to embrace him, James stretches out his arms but finds nothing; he hears Jesus say 'Know and embrace me!', which Böhlig reasonably suggests is intended to express the idea that it is not the stretching out of the hands but gnosis which brings one to Jesus. Accordingly James rejoices (57.10 ff.).

James continues his speech, now directly addressing his judges. Condemned to death, he is flung down from the pinnacle of the Temple (cf. Euseb. HE ii.23) and stoned. The document ends with his dying prayer (62.12 ff.). The points of interest in this text are obviously first the connections with Jewish Christianity already noted, and the use which is made of them in a Gnostic context; and secondly the frequent New Testament echoes and allusions; but there are also affinities with the martyrdoms in some of the apocryphal Acts. Here again detailed comparisons have still to be made.

The last of the documents to be considered in the present context is the *Apocalypse of Adam*. In contrast to the three preceding texts, which all have a distinct Christian colouring, this document shows at most only slight traces of Christian influence, and indeed in Böhlig's opinion derives from a pre-Christian Gnosis. Here lies its significance, for if Böhlig is correct we now have for the first time a genuine document of this Gnosis.

Externally, it is a revelation transmitted by Adam and his son Seth 'in the 700th year', which Böhlig takes to be the 700th year of Seth's life, 100 years before the death of Adam (Gen. 5.1–5). This revelation however contains within itself an account of a revelation made *to Adam* by three men, with whom Böhlig compares the three men who appeared to Abraham at Mamre on the one hand (Gen. 18.1), and the three Uthras of Mandeism on the other. Böhlig's analysis of the contents is as follows:

Introduction 64.2–4.
I. Adam's account of his own and Eve's experiences 64.5–67.14.
II. The Apocalypse proper 67.14–85.15.
  1. The Flood as an attack upon all mankind; preservation of the Men of Seth and of Noah 67.22–73.24.
  2. The destruction by fire as an attack on the Men of Seth and their dependants, and their preservation 73.25–76.7.
  3. The coming of the Phoster for the deliverance of the Sons of Noah 76.8–77.27.
  Excursus: The fourteen statements about the origin of the Phoster 77.27–83.4.
  4. Repentance of the Peoples and sentence of judgment 83.4–85.18.
  Conclusion 85.19–31.

Part I, relating the experiences of Adam and Eve, again falls into three sections, each of which speaks first of a manifestation of glory and then of an act of the Demiurge. In the first, Adam and Eve walk in glory, like the great eternal angels, and are taught 'a word of gnosis of God the eternal'. It is expressly stated that they were superior to the Demiurge, 'higher than the God who created us, and the angels that were with him', and he in his wrath divides them—Böhlig here aptly cites the Gospel of Philip (71, 78). This leads to the loss both of glory and of gnosis. The gnosis does not however perish, but passes into a new race of men, 'the seed of great aeons'.

Having lost the eternal gnosis of the true God, Adam and Eve are now instructed concerning dead works, come to know the God who made them (i.e. the Demiurge) and serve him in fear and slavery. In his sleep, three men appear to Adam—who do not belong to the powers of the Demiurge. They arouse him from the sleep of death, but the Demiurge takes note. The text here is damaged, but among his devices apparently is the creation of sexual desire. Weakness falls upon man, and the days of his life are shortened. Adam recognises that he is now come under the power of death. Now he will proclaim to Seth the revelation given him by the three. The theme is the promise of salvation, and the discourse describes the way in which the race of Seth, with those others who confess him, will be preserved and delivered from harm. The whole section is cast in the future tense, for this is after all an apocalypse. For present purposes however it will be more convenient to use the present throughout. An interesting feature here is the use of the Old Testament history in a *Gnostic* apocalypse.

First the Demiurge (here called the Pantocrator) brings a flood to destroy all flesh and in particular those to whom the revelation of gnosis had come down (i.e. through Seth). The plan is thwarted, because angels descend and carry them off in clouds (cf. AJ 73.4 ff. Till on Noah). Then the Demiurge will relent and take pity on Noah (expressly identified with Deucalion), and in conformity with the Biblical account set him and his family on the land. The men of Seth, who 'were separated through the knowledge of the great aeons and the angels', once more make their appearance, which arouses the wrath of the Demiurge. Noah protests his innocence, and they are then apparently brought into a land appropriate for them, where they build a holy dwelling-place.

Noah now divides the earth among his sons, Shem, Ham and Japhet, urging upon them and their seed obedience to the Pantocrator. But 400,000 men of the seed of Ham and Japhet join with the men of gnosis, and these are protected from all evil works and unclean desire.

The seed of Ham and Japhet now form twelve kingdoms, and call on the Demiurge (here called Saklas), emphasising that the seed of Noah has fulfilled his will, but that the race of Seth with its allies has not. The Demiurge now sends his powers to destroy them with fire. (Here as at other points Böhlig notes Mandean parallels, but surely both the Mandeans and these Gnostics are dependent on the Old Testament (the Flood, Sodom and Gomorrah)? It is of course at some distance.) Once again the men of gnosis are delivered.

The third epoch brings on the scene the figure of the *Phoster*, who comes to deliver men sunk in the power of death. This word had already occurred on the previous page (75.14 f.), where it seems to refer to the heavenly luminaries. It is after all the word used in Genesis (1.14) for the two great lights in the firmament (cf. also the four great lights in the Apocryphon of John 33.1 ff. Till. The Codex II version uses the Greek word here). He does signs and wonders, which alarm the Demiurge, who stirs up wrath against him. And, it is said, 'the glory will come and dwell in holy houses which it has chosen for itself' (is this an echo of Paul's 'temples of the Holy Spirit'?). The powers cannot see him, hence they punish his fleshly manifestation (cf. Asc. Is. 9.14 f.).

This is the point at which we must call a halt. Böhlig remarks that at first one might think of an allusion to the sufferings of Jesus, but goes on to observe that this would be the only mention of Jesus in the text, and that even here the name is not once mentioned. Hence he thinks the assumption of a pre-Christian idea nearer to hand, and turns to Iranian religion, which 'definitely exercised an influence on the late-Jewish Gnosis'.[77]

Three points may be raised in objection, although Böhlig's argument has convinced at least one scholar:[78] first, that the narrative, brief and summary as it is, appears too closely tailored to the figure of Jesus to be entirely independent; second, that there is, as already noted, something that looks very like a New Testament echo in this very passage; and third, that at the close of the treatise there is a reference to 'the holy baptism of those who know the eternal gnosis through the logos-born (*logogenes*) and the incorruptible *phosteres* which have come forth from the holy seed, Jesseus, /Maz/areus, /Jesse/dekeus . . .' Jesseus Maza-reus—thus restored by Böhlig—might well be a corruption of Iesous Nazareus, and I suspect that Jessedekeus might originally have had something to do with Melchizedek. The Christian element is certainly slight, but is it completely non-existent? Böhlig himself draws attention to Revelation 12.5–6 as a parallel to 78.18 ff.—which speaks of a virgin mother and her child driven into the wilderness. But as already noted in an earlier chapter he prefers to think of the mythology lying behind Revelation. In any case, if it *is* from Revelation, it has been thoroughly worked over! Moreover, we need some further information about the Iranian parallels to which Böhlig appeals, their date and so forth. For if they are first attested in comparatively late Iranian texts they cannot be called into account here. In short, this is an interesting but not yet absolutely certain suggestion.

[77] ibid., p. 58.
[78] Cf. G. W. MacRae, *Heythrop Journal* 6, (1965), pp. 27 ff. See also Böhlig in *Oriens Christianus* 48, (1964), pp. 44 ff.

The text is in fact a curious mixture—we have references to Deucalion and the Pierides, together with Sodom and Gomorrah, the Flood, and Solomon apparently rather out of context. It is clearly a witness to a syncretism no longer controlled by exact knowledge of the texts, and recalls the eagerness of native guides to associate all kinds of events with their own particular sites. In view of this, and of the Mandean and other parallels to which Böhlig has drawn attention, I should be inclined (but very tentatively!) to disagree with him and suggest that this document represents not a pre-Christian Gnosis but a later stage.[79] This however is a question which remains to be explored.

And what shall I more say? For the time would fail me—these ancient words are still apposite, especially when there is such a mass of material to discuss, and more yet to come. Yet perhaps even so cursory and superficial account may serve to indicate something of the significance of these texts, and of the tasks that still await attention.

[79] More confidently Schenke in *OLZ* 61, (1966), col. 32.

Epilogue and Conclusion

THE discussion of the question of definition, in the first chapter, had already been drafted before the appearance of two recent contributions by H. M. Schenke, in which he also deals with the question, but from a somewhat different angle of approach.[1] Comparison may serve to show the extent of our agreement, and to bring the points at issue into sharper focus.

1. In the first place, Schenke uses the term Gnosis for preference, rather than Gnosticism, and he includes under this head the following figures or groups:

a. Simon Magus, Menander, Cerinthus, Saturnilus, Basilides, Valentinus, Marcion, Mani, with their respective disciples and adherents.

b. the Carpocratians; the Naassenes, Peratae and Sethians (in Hippolytus); the Nicolaitans, Ophites, Sethians and others (in Epiphanius); the Ophians in Origen; the Gnostics of Plotinus; the Mandeans.

c. two systems in Irenaeus, *Adv. haer.* i.29 and 30 (27 and 28 Harvey); the Gnostic Justin; the Poimandres and other Hermetic documents; Coptic Gnostic texts.

From this it will immediately be evident that for Schenke Gnosis is both wider than Gnosticism as defined above, and narrower than Gnosis in the wider and vaguer sense in which the term has been used in this book. On closer inspection it will be seen that Schenke's Gnosis, as here defined, is the 'classical' Gnosticism with the addition in group (a) of Marcion and Mani, in group (b) of the Mandeans and in group (c) of the Hermetica. All of these, beyond question, must be taken into account in any comprehensive treatment of the question, but as we have seen there is reason for some reserve about classifying Marcion as a Gnostic without qualification; Schenke himself speaks of Manicheism as a second major wave of the Gnostic movement, swamping the older systems;[2] the precise relation of the Her-

[1] *Kairos* 2, (1965), pp. 114 ff.; *Umwelt des Christentums*, i, (Berlin 1965), pp. 371 ff.
[2] *Kairos*, p. 121.

metica to Gnosticism in the strict sense is not yet fully settled; and finally Schenke himself traces a three-stage development of the Mandeans, who were originally a heretical Jewish Baptist sect, exposed *at a second stage* to the Gnostic *Weltanschauung*.[3] Both Manicheism and Mandeism are important for the understanding of the nature of the Gnostic phenomenon, and may legitimately be drawn upon to *illustrate* the significance of terms and concepts in the earlier Gnosticism and even in the New Testament. There is however an ever-present danger (of which Schenke is fully aware) that such illustration may pass over into derivation, that in words already quoted parallels may be converted into influences and influences into sources. Both Manicheism and Mandeism present enough in the way of distinctive features of their own to be classed apart, as related to but still to some extent distinct from the systems of the second century. It is for this reason among others that the wider definition of Gnosis has been employed above, and these two groups included under it.

A second point of difference relates to the inclusion of Simon Magus in group (a). This of course has the authority of Irenaeus in support, but how far is it true to say that Simon himself taught in Samaria in the first half of the first Christian century 'a typically Gnostic *Weltanschauung*'?[4] How much of the developed Simonian system known to Irenaeus was actually held by Simon himself, and how much was fathered upon him by later adherents? To ascribe to Simon a developed Gnostic system *may* be to read back Gnosticism into a period earlier than is justified by the texts at our disposal.

2. Negatively, Schenke affirms that Gnosis is not a degenerate Christianity, as Harnack held; nor is it the direct continuation of an oriental (or Iranian) popular religion, as maintained by the school of *Religionsgeschichte* and their modern adherents; nor is it simply the spirit of late antiquity, as Jonas holds. On the first two points here we are in complete agreement, but on the third the wider definition given in this book to the term Gnosis brings us closer to the position of Jonas. Schenke would no doubt claim that this wider definition is too vague to be of any value, but the fact remains that we require some term by which

[3] *Umwelt*, p. 401. See the whole excursus pp. 396 ff., and cf. above, p. 14 f.
[4] *Kairos*, p. 130.

to describe the whole complex of phenomena which show some affinity with Gnosticism proper but cannot yet be considered fully Gnostic in the second-century sense. Moreover Schenke himself goes on to claim that his Gnosis came into being shortly before Christianity or coevally with it, but independently of it, and traces its origins to unorthodox and unofficial Jewish circles in the pre-Christian period.

3. At first sight there is some inconsistency between Schenke's statement[5] that a derivation of Gnosis from Judaism is no better or more plausible than any other derivation, from Christianity or Hellenism, from Egypt or from Persia, and his subsequent argument[6] that Jewish people had a fundamental share in the origins of Gnosticism and in its earliest dissemination. This however is a situation familiar to anyone who has tried to write about the subject. The Jewish contribution to Gnosticism is unmistakable, as we have seen, and it is therefore probable that Jews had some part in the process of development. But Gnosis and Gnosticism are not to be derived from Judaism alone, for other cultures also have made their contribution. And we have the problem raised by Jonas:[7] what could have led Jews to trample on all that was holy in their ancestral faith? Schenke suggests the reaction of an unofficial group to persecution by their 'orthodox' neighbours, but other explanations are also possible.

Schenke rightly notes the possibility that certain Jewish elements in Christian Gnostic systems may have found their way thither through the medium of Christianity, but where the Christian elements are often a mere veneer the Jewish are generally integral to the system.[8] Here the discussion of the Nag Hammadi documents in the two preceding chapters may suggest that we can make a distinction within Gnosticism proper between those systems and documents which are only superficially Christianised, and hence admit the hypothesis of a non-Christian Jewish-Gnostic basis, and those in which the Christian elements are more fundamental. Generalisation here could be misleading, since what is true of the one group may not be true of the other. Non-Christian, moreover, need not necessarily mean pre-Christian.

<hr>

[5] ibid., p. 125.   [6] ibid., p. 133.
[7] *The Bible in Modern Scholarship*, pp. 289 f.   [8] *Kairos*, p. 127.

Schenke places the origin of his Gnosis shortly before or contemporary with the rise of Christianity. The discussion in previous chapters of this book has recognised the existence of trends and tendencies in this period which have been classed as Gnosis in the wider sense, or perhaps better as pre-Gnosis. Examination of the New Testament evidence takes us back at least to the last quarter of the first century for the first signs of incipient Gnosticism, and there are indications, although the question is much debated, that the beginnings of the movement go back still further; but the process of transition from Gnosis (or pre-Gnosis) to Gnosticism proper is still obscure.

Not all investigators into the problems of Gnosis and Gnosticism would entirely agree with all the positions noted in this discussion, but the extent of the agreement between two scholars of differing training, background and approach may perhaps suggest that a consensus of opinion on these questions is not so remote a prospect as is sometimes thought.

To sum up: the problems of Gnosticism, and in particular the problem of Gnostic origins, are more complex than is sometimes recognised. Particular motifs and concepts can be traced far back into the pre-Christian period, but it is not clear that such motifs can be truly classed as Gnostic except in the context of the developed Gnostic systems. Attempts to derive the whole movement from any single source come to grief, for no one of the various theories propounded is completely adequate. Moreover, as Schenke notes,[9] Gnosticism (or on his definition Gnosis) is not merely the sum of its constituent elements. We have to take account also of the fact stressed by Jonas, and others after him, that here we have a new attitude, a new outlook upon life, a radical acosmism which repudiates this world and man's existence in it. Gnosticism is not however a religion of despair, for it offers a hope in the prospect, for the elect at least, of return to the realm of light to which man essentially belongs.

The Jewish element in the developed Gnosticism is unmistakable. In some of our documents the Christian element appears to be only a superficial veneer, whereas the Jewish is integral to the whole. Again, there are cases, as with the Hermetica and Mandeism, in which we find theories of a Gnostic type with Jewish elements but little if any sign of

[9] ibid., p. 126.

Christian influence. These and other facts suggest that the earliest beginnings of the movement are to be sought in Jewish circles, probably in Palestine or Syria rather than Alexandria, for there are Jewish elements in Gnosticism of which there is no trace in Philo. If this be so, the Iranian and Mesopotamian elements may have been mediated through Judaism, and the contribution of Greek philosophy may belong to a later stage of the development; but here we are largely in the realm of speculation.

Christianity emerged on the stage of history in much the same period. It is therefore reasonable to assume that the factors which promoted the development of Gnosticism also had some influence on the emergent Christian faith. Such influence however need not have operated in the same way, or produced the same results. We have to note the differences as well as the similarities.

A further question is that of the stage at which Christianity and Gnosis came into contact, whether it was already early in the New Testament period or only later. Here there has been a widespread tendency to speak of Gnostic influence upon the New Testament, but the fact is that at a later stage the Gnostics were to adopt and adapt the New Testament to their own ends. The influence therefore was not altogether on the one side, and it would be better to envisage a period of mutual interpenetration and interaction. Here an analogy used by A. M. Hunter[10] may be relevant: Shakespeare, he writes, 'is indebted to the past in every play. His plots he often took from others. Now he recast an old play, now he turned to Plutarch or to Holinshed. Yet, though he borrowed, though in a score of ways he owed a debt to the past, Shakespeare stands out, unapproached and unapproachable, as the most original literary genius in the English language.'

This analogy is capable of wider application. In our present context, it is not the ultimate source of a theme or concept which finally matters, but the use that is made of it. And it is here that the distinctive character of the New Testament and Christian tradition, over against the Gnostic, begins to emerge. Paul, for example, can accept the contemporary *Weltanschauung* of his time, but he rejects the Gnostic interpretation of it. It is

[10] *Paul and his Predecessors*, (London 1961), p. 113.

right and proper to set the New Testament in the context of its contemporary environment, to study its documents in the light of what we can learn about the world of that time; but we must beware of drawing the wrong conclusions from our study. Gnosticism is another response to the problems of the age, at some points in close agreement with Christianity, but at others completely at variance. A balanced assessment of their mutual relationships must give to each its due.

Index

The more important references are shown in bold type.